STOP TUBERCULOSIS - HERBAL APPROACH

SACHIN C NARWADIYA

Made with ♥ on the Notion Press Platform
www.notionpress.com

The book is dedicated the sufferrer of Tuberculosis and their families.................

Contents

Acknowledgements

Thanks to almighty who by grace and mercy bestowed upon me the opportunity and strength to complete my research work under the able and valuable guidance of learned Professor Dr. V. G. Meshram, P. G. Department of Biochemistry, and Dr. P. M. Tumane, Reader, P.G. Department of Microbiology at R.T.M Nagpur University, Nagpur (M.S) India. I am indebted to them for the interest and pains taken by them for completion of my thesis that spread over the period from 2004-2009 and later on 2013-2014.

It would be an ingratitude if I do not express my thanks to the Late Dr. S. U. Meshram, Professor and Ex-Head, P.G. Department of Microbiology, R.T.M Nagpur University, Nagpur (M.S) India, for obliging me with the permission and facilities provided for, in absence of which the research work would not have been done as standard work in my opinion.

I extend my gratitude to Dr. B. J. Wader, Professor and Head, P.G. Department of Microbiology, R.T.M Nagpur University, Nagpur (M.S) India, for regular encouragement during my work. I am thankful to B. B. Mandal, Senior Research Officer, National Institute of Miners' Health for his constant encouragement at each and every step of the said study.

I am thankful to Dr. (Mrs) Sandhya V. Saoji, Microbiologist, for her constant support and valuable advice for successfully performing all anti TB tests, preparation of L. J. Medium and interpretation for the results. I am thankful to Dr. K. V. Shankhapal, and Dr. A. O. Ingle, P. G. Department of Microbiology, R.T.M Nagpur University, Nagpur.(M.S) India.

I am very much thankful to Dr. S. S. Pande, Dr. (Mrs) A. S. Shanware, Rajiv Gandhi Biotechnology Centre, R.T.M Nagpur University, Nagpur (M.S) India for time to time help, suggestions and encouragement during my research work.

Special thanks to Ex-Director, National Institute of Miners' Health Dr. S. K. Dave for permitting me for registration for the above study. I am much indebted to Dr. Nirmalendu Nath and Dr. Shiv Kumar Chauhan for obliged me by giving his support during the compiling of work. I am very much thankful to Mr. Umesh Dhumne, Senior Scientific Assistant, National Institute of Miners' Health, for helping me in the statistical analysis of the data generated in this study with Epi Info software.

I also thanks to Dr. N. M. Dongarwar, P. G. Department of Botany, R.T.M Nagpur University, Nagpur (M.S) India for identification and authentication of plant species. I am also thankful to my colleagues Mr. Keertisheel Sahare, Mr. Alok Rai, Ms. Nasreen Jan, and all the non-teaching staff of P.G. Department of Microbiology and Rajiv Gandhi Biotechnology Centre, R.T.M Nagpur University, Nagpur (M.S) India.

I wish to offer my thanks to Dr. R. Gopichnadran, Director and Dr. T. V. Venketswaran, Academic Head, at Vigyan Prasar, Department of Science and Technology, Government of India, New Delhi highly obliged me by their suggestions to compilation of the work.

I wish to place my profound gratitude Dr. Irfana Begum, Project Officer, EduSAT, Vigyan Prasar, Department of Science and Technology, Government of India, New Delhi for her invaluable criticism and suggestions.

I wish to offer my special thanks to Dr Shardul Wagh for his constant support in writing thesis with his valuable comments.

It would be ingratitude if I don't remember an honor Dr. Haroon H. Marikar, for compilation of work. At the end I feel no hitch to accept that I am fortune enough that my parents and members of my family, wife, children, friends provided me all that I needed for my research work, and their moral support, good blessings and well wishes to carry out this work.

I am thankful to my friends Mr. Pravin Dombde, Dr. S. Shahzad, Dr. Imran Sadi, Dr. F. Ahmad, Mr. Dattatray Kanitkar, Ms. Nazneen A. Shaikh, Ms. Mona Bhattad, Ms. A. Kathale, Mrs. Shilpa Ingole for their constant encouragement for the successful completion of the study.

I would like to extend my warm thanks to the all the members of NIMH and Vigyan Prasar for their direct and indirect support for completion of the work.

In the end I would not lack behind in thanking and tending my sincere gratitude to those person who co-operated during my research work by all means.

(Sachin C. Narwadiya)

CHAPTER ONE

ABBREVATIONS

• Ab	Antibody
• Ag	Antigen
• ACSM	advocacy, communication and social mobilization activities
• AIDS	Acquired Immuno Disease Syndrome
• AFB	Acid Fast Bacilli
• ART	Anti-Retroviral Therapy
• ARTI	Annual Risk of TB Infection
• BCG	Bacillus Calmatte Guarine
• CFA	Component of Freund's complete Adjuvant
• CFP	Culture Filtrate Proteins
• CPT	co-trimoxazole preventive therapy
• DOTS	Directly Observed Short Term Treatment
• DR	Drug Resistant
• DRS	Drug Resistance Surveillance
• DST	Drug Susceptibility Testing
• DTC	District Tuberculosis Centre
• *E.coli*	*Escherichia coli*
• ETH	Ethambutol
• EQA	External Quality Assessment
• ESI	Employees State Insurance
• GLC	Green Light Committee
• HBCs	High Burden Countries
• HIV	Human Immunodeficiency Virus
• i.e	That is

• IUAT	International Union Against Tuberculosis
• IUATLD	International Union Against Tuberculosis and Lung Disease
• KDa	Kilo-dalton
• L.J Medium	Lowenstein Jensen's Medium
• MDR-TB	Multi Drug Resistant Tuberculosis
• MTB	*Mycobacterium tuberculosis*
• NACP	National AIDS Control Programme
• NGOs	Non-Governmental Organizations
• NSP	New Smear Positive
• NTP	National Tuberculosis Programme
• PAS	p-amino salicylic acid
• PIS	Patient's Isolated Strains
• PMN	Polymorphonuclear
• PPD	Purified Protein Derivative
• PPM	public–private mix
• Ref	Reference
• RNTCP	Revised National Tuberculosis Control Programme
• RTM	Rashtrasant Tukadoji Maharaj
• SSM	Standard Strain of *Mycobacterium tuberculosis*
• TB	Tuberculosis
• TPIS	Tuberculosis Programme Information System
• UNAIDS	United Nations Programme on Acquired Immuno Disease Syndrome
• US	United States
• VCTC	Voluntary Counseling and Testing Centers
• WHA	World Health Assembly
• WHO	World Health Organization
• XDR	Extensively Drug Resistant

CHAPTER TWO

Introduction

Diseases are as old as mankind. As long as human existed there were disease and they were attributed to curse from God. There are many diseases and infections that debilitate health and well being of humans. These include chicken pox, diphtheria, tuberculosis, acquired immune deficiency syndrome (AIDS) and so on. The sufferings of human being due to the diseases inspired scientists and researchers to develop or invent treatment using active compounds extracted from various sources as plants, fungi to fight against diseases or infections.

A disease is an abnormal condition that affects the body of an organism. It may be caused by factors that originate from an external source, such as infectious disease, or it may be caused by internal dysfunctions, such as autoimmune diseases. In humans, "disease" is often used more broadly to refer to any condition that causes pain, dysfunction, distress, social problems, or death to the person afflicted, or similar problems for those in contact with the affected person. In this broader sense, it includes injuries, disabilities, disorders, syndromes, infections, isolated symptoms, deviant behaviours, and atypical variations of structure and function. In other contexts these may be include distinct categories. Diseases usually affect people not only physically, but also emotionally, as contracting and living with many diseases can alter one's perspective on life, and one's personality.

Accordingly there are four main types of disease: pathogenic, deficiency related, hereditary, and physiological. They could also be either communicable or non-communicable. The deadliest disease in humans is ischemic heart disease (blood flow obstruction), followed by cerebro-vascular disease and lower respiratory infections respectively.

This condition of disease was first recognized by Hippocrates around 460 B.C. He used the term phthisis to introduced tuberculosis in ancient Greek. In his Book *"Of the Epidemics"*, he described the characteristics of the disease: fever, colorless urine, coughs resulting in a thick sputa, and loss of thirst and appetite. He noted that most people who suffered became delirious before they succumbed to the disease. According to him, this disease typically affected individuals between 18 and 35 and was nearly always fatal. He forbids physicians from visiting victims of the disease to protect their reputation.

At the same time Aristotle believed that the disease might be contagious while another companion opined that symptoms of this disease are hereditary. Galen, the most eminent Greek physician after Hippocrates, defined phthisis as the "ulceration of the lungs, thorax or throat, accompanied by a cough, fever, and consumption of the body by pus. Galen proposed a series of therapeutic treatments for the disease, including: opium as a sleeping agent and painkiller; blood letting; a diet of barley water, fish, and fruit. He also described the phyma (tumor) of the lungs, thought to correspond to tubercles that form on the lung as a result of the disease.

Tuberculosis was first described by Silvius, in his book Opera Medica in 1679. It is not until 1720 that the history of tuberculosis starts to take shape as we understand today as the physician Benjamin Marten describes in his "A Theory of Consumption" that tuberculosis may be caused by small living creatures transmitted through air to other patients. Despite these breakthroughs, the disease still presented a nearly impossible battle for most patients until at least the mid nineteenth century.

The detailed study of the causative agents of the diseases is helpful in understanding of disease pattern and the approach for treatment. Over the past decades tuberculosis remained the focus for treatment. The causative agent for tuberculosis is *Mycobacterium tuberculosis.* Hence its morphology, life cycle briefly explained for understanding of the disease.

Stages of the Disease:-

Stage 1

Droplet nuclei are inhaled. Droplet nuclei are generated during talking coughing and sneezing. Coughing generates about 3000 droplet nuclei. Talking for 5 minutes generates 3000 droplet nuclei but singing generates 3000 droplet nuclei in one minute. Sneezing generates the most droplet nuclei by far, that can spread to individuals up to 10 feet away.

Stage 2

It begins 7-21 days after initial infection. *Mycobacterium tuberculosis* multiplies virtually unrestricted within inactivated macrophages until the macrophages burst. Other macrophages also phagocytose *Mycobacterium tuberculosis*. They are howeverinactivated and hence can not destroy *Mycobacterium tuberculosis*.

Stage 3

At this stage lymphocytes begin to infiltrate. The lymphocytes, specifically T-cells, recognize processed and presented *Mycobacterium tuberculosis* antigen in context of MHC (Major Histocompatibility complex) molecules. This results in T-cell activation and the liberation of cytokines including gamma interferon (IFN). The liberation of IFN causes the activation of macrophages. These activated macrophages are now capable of destroying *Mycobacterium tuberculosis*.

At this stage that tubercle formation begins. The center of the tubercle is characterized by "cessation necrosis" meaning semi-solid or "cheesy" consistency. *Mycobacterium tuberculosis* cannot multiply within these tubercles because of the low pH and anoxic environment. *Mycobacterium tuberculosis* can, however, persist within these tubercles for extended periods.

Stage 4

The growing tubercle may invade a bronchus. If this happens, *Mycobacterium tuberculosis* infection can spread to other parts of the lung. Similarly the tubercle may invade an artery or other blood supply line. The hematogenous spread of *Mycobacterium tuberculosis* may result in extra-pulmonary tuberculosis otherwise known as milliary tuberculosis.The name "milliary" is derived from the fact that metastasizing tubercles are about the same size as a millet seed, a grain commonly grown in Africa.

The secondary lesions caused by milliary TB can occur at almost any anatomical location, but usually involve the genitourinary system, bones, joints, lymph nodes, and peritoneum.

These lesions are of two types:

1. Exudative lesionsresult from the accumulation of PMN's around *Mycobacterium tuberculosis*. The bacteria replicate with virtually no resistance. This situation gives rise to the formation of a "soft tubercle".

2. Productive or granulomatouslesionsoccur when the host becomes hypersensitive to tuberculo-proteins. This situation gives rise to the formation of a "hard tubercle".

Mycobacterium tuberculosis

Mycobacterium tuberculosis is a fairly large non-motile rod-shaped bacterium distantly related to the Actinomycetes. Many non pathogenic mycobacteria are components of the normal flora of humans, found most often in dry and oily locales. The rods are 2-4 μm in length and 0.2-0.5 μm in width.

Mycobacterium tuberculosis is an obligate aerobe. For this reason, in the classic case of tuberculosis, the *Mycobacterium tuberculosis* complexes are always found in the well-aerated upper lobes of the lungs. The bacterium is a facultative intracellular parasite, usually of macrophages, and has a slow generation time, 15-20 hours, as a physiological characteristic that may contribute to its virulence. Two media are used to grow *Mycobacterium tuberculosis* Middle brook's agar based medium and Lowenstein-Jensen egg based medium. *Mycobacterium tuberculosis* colonies are small and buff colored when grown on either medium. Both media contain inhibitors to prevent contaminants from out-growing *Mycobacterium tuberculosis*. It takes 4-6 weeks to get colonies that are visible on either type of media.

Chains of cells in smears made from *in vitro* grown colonies often form distinctive serpentine cords. This observation was first made by Robert Koch who associated cord factor with virulent strains of the bacterium.

Mycobacterium tuberculosis is not classified as either Gram-positive or Gram-negative because it does not have the chemical characteristics of either, though it contains peptidoglycan (murein) in the cell wall. If a Gram stain is performed on *Mycobacterium tuberculosis* it stains very weakly and is referred as "ghosts". (Hubert Bloch, 1949)

Mycobacterium species, along with members of a related genus Nocardia are classified as acid-fast bacteria due to impermeability by certain dyes and stains. Despite this, once stained, acid-fast bacteria will retain dyes when heated and treated with acidified organic compounds. An acid-fast staining method for *Mycobacterium tuberculosis* is the Ziehl-Neelsen stain. In this method, the *Mycobacterium tuberculosis* smear is fixed and stained with carbol-fuchsin (a pink dye) followed by decolorization with acid-alcohol. Further the smear is counterstained with methylene-blue or picric acid, as a result acid-fast bacilli appear pink in a contrasting blue background.

In order to detect *Mycobacterium tuberculosis* in a sputum sample, in excess of 10,000 organisms per ml of sputum, 100X microscope objective is needed. Acid-fast bacillus/slide is regarded as "suspicious" of a *Mycobacterium tuberculosis* Infection.

The cell wall structure of *Mycobacterium tuberculosis* deserves special attention because it is unique among prokaryotes a major determinant of virulence for the bacterium. The cell wall complex contains peptidoglycan, otherwise composed of complex lipids. Over 60% of the mycobacterial cell wall is lipid. The lipid fraction of *Mycobacterium tuberculosis*'s cell wall consists of three major components namely Mycolic acids, Cord factor and Wax D.

Mycolic acids are unique alpha-branched lipids found in cell walls of *Mycobacterium* and *Corynebacterium*. They make up 50% of the dry weight of the mycobacterial cell envelope. Mycolic acids are strong hydrophobic molecules that form a lipid shell around the organism and affect permeability properties at the cell surface. Mycolic Acids are thought to be a significant determinant of virulence in *Mycobacterium tuberculosis*. Probably, they prevent attack of the mycobacteria by cationic proteins, lysozyme and oxygen radicals in the phagocytic granule. They also protect extra-cellular mycobacteria from complement deposition in serum.

Cord Factor is responsible for the serpentine cording. It has been reported that cord factor plays a fundamental role in the genesis and persistence of the chronic and granulomatous lesions caused by mycobacteria. Virulent strains of the *Mycobacterium tuberculosis* complex (*M. tuberculosis*) often grow as characteristic ropes, bundles, or serpentine cords of acid-fast bacilli (AFB) in liquid media and are influenced by the composition of the culture medium and the conditions of culture. (F. Zuhre Badak *et al.*1999) Cord factor is toxic to mammalian cells and inhibits PMN migration. Cord factor is most abundantly produced in virulent strains of *Mycobacterium tuberculosis*.

(http://encyclopedia2.thefreedictionary.com/cord+factor[online], accessed on 10-05-2014)

Wax D fraction extracted from human tubercle bacilli is a macromolecular peptide-glycolipid consisting of mycolic acid, polysaccharide, and peptide. Wax D fraction obtained from human tubercle bacilli showed characteristic biological adjuvant activity in the immune response, induction of adjuvant arthritis in rats (I Azuma *et al*, 1968). Wax-D in the cell envelope is the major component of Freund's complete adjuvant (CFA). Due to the presence of high concentration of lipids in the cell wall of *Mycobacterium tuberculosis,* the bacterium acquire following properties.

- Impermeability to stains and dyes
- Resistance to many antibiotics
- Resistance to killing by acidic and alkaline compounds
- Resistance to osmotic lysis via complement deposition

General properties of *Mycobacterium tuberculosis* (MTB) responsible for virulence

Special mechanisms for cell entry:- The tubercle bacillus can bind directly to mannose receptors on macrophages via the cell wall-associated mannosylated glycolipid, LAM, or indirectly via certain complement receptors or Fc receptors.

Intracellular growth:- MTB can grow intracellularly. This is an effective means of evading the immune system. In particular, antibodies and complement are ineffective. Once MTB is phagocytosed, it can inhibit phagosome-lysosome fusion by secretion of a protein that modifies the phagosome membrane. It may remain in the phagosome or escape from the phagosome, in either case, finding a protected environment for growth in the macrophage.

Detoxification of oxygen radicals:- MTB interferes with the toxic effects of reactive oxygen intermediates produced in the process of phagocytosis by three mechanisms:

1. Compounds including glycolipids, sulfatides and LAM down regulate the oxidative cytotoxic mechanism.
2. Macrophage uptake via complement receptors may bypass the activation of a respiratory burst.
3. The oxidative burst may be counteracted by production of catalase and superoxide dismutase enzymes.

Antigen 85 complex:- This complex is composed of a group of proteins secreted by MTB known to bind fibronectin. These proteins may aid in walling off the bacteria from the immune system and may facilitate tubercle formation.

Slow generation time:- Because of MTB's slow generation time, the immune system may not readily recognize the bacteria or may not be triggered sufficiently to eliminate them.

Many other chronic diseases are caused by bacteria with slow generation time, for example, slow-growing *M. leprae* causes leprosy, *Treponema pallidum* causes syphilis, and *Borrelia burgdorferi* causes Lyme disease.

High lipid concentration in cell wall: - It accounts for impermeability and resistance to antimicrobial agents, resistance to killing by acidic and alkaline compounds in both the intracellular and extra-cellular environment, and resistance to osmotic lysis via complement deposition and attack by lysozyme.

Cord factor. Cord factor (trehalose 6, 6' dimycolate) is a glycolipid found in the cell walls of mycobacteria, which causes the cells to grow in serpentine cords. It is primarily associated with virulent strains of MTB. It is known to be toxic to mammalian cells and to be an inhibitor of PMN migration. Its exact role in MTB virulence is unclear, although it has been shown to induce granulomatous reactions identical to those seen in TB. *M. tuberculosis* virulence is studied both in tissue culture, using macrophages, dendritic cells or pneumocytes, and in animal models, primarily mice. Tissue culture models are easier to work with and give faster results, but they are limited to studying early stages of infection. Ultimately, only in animal models can all the stages of TB be studied. Since sequencing the *Mycobacterium tuberculosis* genome in 1998, genetic methods are more commonly used to study the bacterium's virulence. The usual genetic approaches to study virulence are to disrupt, inactivate, modify, delete or complement a gene and assess the effects in the macrophage or mouse model. (Smith I, 2003)

In an exhaustive and comprehensive review of possible virulence determinants of *Mycobacterium tuberculosis* identified four culture filtrate enzymes, eleven cell surface proteins, four groups of enzymes involved in cellular metabolism (including lipid metabolism, amino acid and purine biosynthesis, metal uptake, anaerobic respiration and oxidative stress) and three sets of transcriptional regulators to which some degree of the organism's virulence might be attributed.

Of approximately 4,000 genes in the *Mycobacterium tuberculosis* genome, 525 are involved in cell wall and "cell processes", 188 genes encode regulatory proteins, and 91 genes involved in "virulence, detoxification and adaptation". Over 200 genes are identified as encoding enzymes for the metabolism of fatty acids. This large number of *M. tuberculosis* enzymes that putatively use fatty acids may be related to the ability of the pathogen to grow in the tissues of the infected host, where fatty acids may be the major carbon source. This is thought to be an important aspect of *M. tuberculosis* physiology during infection.

The point is that these genes, as well as those from other classes, may be directly or indirectly involved in virulence. Some of these genes and their products or activities are described below.

Erp:- Erp is a surface-located protein secreted by *M. tuberculosis*. The protein is similar to an exported 28kDa antigen (the PLGTS antigen) in *M. leprae* and is not found in nonpathogenic mycobacteria. Its function in virulence is unknown.

Mas:- *Mas* encodes mycocerosic aid synthase, an enzyme that catalyzes the synthesis of long-chain, multiply methylated branched fatty acids, called mycocerosic acids, that are found only in pathogenic mycobacteria.

FbpA:- Mycobacteria have three mycolyl-transferase enzymes, encoded by three genes, *fbpA*, *fbpB*, and *fbpC*, that transfer long-chain mycolic acids to trehalose derivatives. The proteins can also bind the cell matrix protein fibronectin. The Fbp proteins are also found in the culture filtrate and are known as the antigen 85A, 85B, and 85C complex (Antigen 85 complex).

The three *fbp* genes have been separately inactivated, but only the *M. tuberculosis fbpA* mutant showed severely attenuated growth in human and murine macrophages. The observation that these proteins produce a formidable immunologic response led to the creation of a new live vaccine that was made by introducing the *M. tuberculosis fbpB* gene into *M. bovis* BCG. This recombinant strain shows better protection against virulent *M. tuberculosis* infection than does the parent BCG strain in a guinea pig model.

OmpA :- OmpA is a porin-like protein that can form pores in liposomes, a general property of porin family proteins. *ompA* expression is induced by low pH, as well as by engulfment into macrophages. An *ompA* mutant demonstrated the following phenotypes: although it showed delayed growth at acid pH, it ultimately grew to wild-type levels; could not take up small molecules like serine at low pH; and showed reduced ability to grow in both human and murine macrophages. This suggested that the environment encountered by *M. tuberculosis* during infection is acidic, and that OmpA played a role in the bacterial response to this condition.

HbhA:- HbhA is a heparin-binding hemagglutin protein, localized on the surface of virulent mycobacteria. HbhA mutants exhibited wild-type ability to be phagocytosed by and grow in murine or human macrophages. They are taken up poorly by pneumocytic cells, although the bacterial generation time was normal intracellularly. The mutant grew normally in the lungs of infected mice but had a longer generation time and reached a lower bacterial load in spleens compared to the wild-type. The properties of this mutant indicate that HbhA is important for *M. tuberculosis* interaction with pneumocytes and that this interaction may play a role in extra-pulmonary dissemination.

LAM:- LAM is a complex glycolipid that contains repeating arabinose-mannose disaccharide subunits. It is a major component of the *M. tuberculosis* cell wall. It is known to be an immuno-modulator analogous to the 19-kDa protein. Addition of LAM to murine macrophages depresses IFN-gamma production. LAM can also scavenge oxygen radicals, in vitro, and inhibits the host protein kinase C. It has been suggested that LAM functions to down-regulate host immune responses to *M. tuberculosis* infection, to protect the bacterium from potentially lethal mechanisms like the respiratory burst.

MbtB:- The *mbt* operon, consisting of *mbtA through mbtJ*, encodes enzymes whose function is to synthesize mycobactin and carboxymycobactin, the major siderophores produced by *M. tuberculosis*. The operon is part of a regulon that is repressed in high iron conditions. MbtB is an enzyme that catalyzes an essential step in mycobactin synthesis. Like many other bacterial pathogens, during infection, *Mycobacterium tuberculosis* requires an iron acquisition system consisting of siderophores, to obtain iron from host iron-containing proteins such as transferrin and lactoferrin. Iron is essential for growth of the bacteria and so the element must be extracted from protein-bound iron in the host or from largely insoluble ferric salts in the environment. Iron uptake systems are required to mobilize these forms of iron for transport into the cell. In bacteria, siderophores usually perform this chelation and solubilization function, and the iron they carry is taken into cells by high-affinity iron transport systems.

Oxidative stress proteins:- Most aerobic organisms have enzymes that degrade peroxides and superoxide, which are normal byproducts of aerobic respiration, but also are toxic oxygen radicals. These enzymes, generally superoxide dismutases, catalases and peroxidases, are also important for the response to various external oxidative stresses. Since phagocytic cells produce oxygen radicals during the respiratory burst to kill invading bacteria, it is not surprising that these enzymes may contribute to *M. tuberculosis* virulence. Enzymes found in *M. tuberculosis* that combat oxygen radicals include AhpC, an alkyl hydroperoxide reductase that detoxifies organic hydroxyperoxides, and SodA and SodC, two species of superoxide dismutase that degrade superoxides. The latter are normal by-products of aerobic respiration; also produced by the phagocytic respiratory burst.

Nitrate reductase:- *M. tuberculosis* was originally thought to be an obligate aerobe, but there are numerous experimental indicators that the bacterium can grow in micro-areophilic environments, especially during the later stages of infection, e.g., in lung granulomas. Wild type *M. tuberculosis* has been shown to possess an inducible nitrate reductase (NarG encoded by *narG*) which allows respiration using NO_3 as a final electron acceptor. If anaerobic or microareophilic growth is an important feature of *M. tuberculosis* physiology during infection, the existence of nitrate reductase could be a significant factor in sustaining growth under these conditions.

Adherence

The specific bacterial adhesions involved in the complex interaction between *M. tuberculosis* and the human host are largely unknown. Nevertheless, some potential adherence factors have been considered, including the heparin-binding hemagglutin (HbhA), a fibronectin-binding protein, and a polymorphic acidic, glycine-rich protein, called PE-PGRS. HbhA is a surface-exposed protein that is involved in binding *Mycobacterium tuberculosis* to epithelial cells but not to phagocytes. It could be involved in extra-pulmonary spread after the initial long-term colonization of the host. Fibronectin-binding proteins (FbpA), first identified as the α-antigen (Antigen 85 complex), can bind to the extra-cellular matrix protein fibronectin in vitro. This property may represent a mechanism of tissue colonization. The surface-exposed PE-PGRS proteins found in *M. tuberculosis* and *Mycobacterium bovis* also show fibronectin-binding properties. It has been shown recently that *Mycobacterium tuberculosis* produces pili during human infection, which could be involved in initial colonization of the host (Alteri *et al.*, 2007). Electron microscope investigations revealed that *M. tuberculosis* produces a dense fibrillar meshwork composed of thin coiled, aggregated fibers resembling pili that extend many microns away from the bacterial surface. These structures have been named *Mycobacterium tuberculosis* pili or MTP. Additionally, biochemical and genetic data demonstrate that *M. tuberculosis* produces pili, whose pilin subunit is encoded by the *Rv3312A* gene. The serum of tuberculosis patients with active TB has been shown to contain IgG antibodies to MTP, which suggests that the structures are produced in vivo during human infection. Furthermore, isolated MTP bind to the extracellular matrix protein laminin in vitro, suggesting that they act as an adhesive and may be an important host colonization factor of *M. tuberculosis.*

Because MTP are produced in vivo, and the *M. tuberculosis* habitat is the human body from which it is transmitted directly from person to person, it is likely that pili play an important role in some aspect of human TB infection. If MTP are proven essential for *M. tuberculosis* to establish infection, as in certain other microbes, the purified MTP could be considered as a vaccine candidate.

(http://textbookofbacteriology.net/tuberculosis_3.html[online]accessed on 14-05-2014)

Taxonomic classification of *Mycobacterium tuberculosis*:-

Kingdom

Bacteria

Phylum

Actinobacteria

Class

Actinobacteria

Order

Actinomycetales

Suborder

Corynebacterineae

Family

Mycobacteriaceae

Genus

Mycobacterium

Species

M. tuberculosis

Binomial name

Mycobacterium tuberculosis

Synonyms

Tubercle bacillus Koch 1882

(http://en.wikipedia.org/wiki/Mycobacterium_tuberculosis[online],accessed on14-05-2014)

Once inhaled, the infectious droplets settle throughout the airways. The majority of the bacilli are trapped in the upper parts of the airways where the mucus-secreting goblet cells exist. The mucus produced catches foreign substances, and the cilia on the surface of the cells constantly beat the mucus and its entrapped particles upward for removal.

ICMR (Indian Council for Medicinal Research) guidelines for anti tuberculosis tests and its diagnosis

There are two basic approaches for the diagnosis of tuberculosis. The direct approach includes detection of *Mycobacteria* or its products and the indirect approach includes measurements of humoral and cellular products of the host against tuberculosis. The diagnosis of tuberculosis in endemic countries depends more on the use of labour intensive, easy to use methodology with minimum infrastructure or equipments. The method of direct smear microscopy has following desirable features: Results within 2 hours, simple training, easy interpretation, function well in HIV (human immunodeficiency virus) positive patients and allows start of treatment as early as possible. Currently less then 20% of the nearly 10 million predicted annual cases of tuberculosis are identified as smear positive.

Direct Approach

Microscopy:-

It is simplest and most rapidly available procedure currently available for the detection of Acid fast bacilli (AFB) by Ziehl-Neelson staining method or its modifications. Fluorescent staining method offers the advantage of screening of the smear under low power where large numbers of slides is screened in less time.

Culture

Isolation of mycobacteria from clinical samples by cultures still is definitive for the diagnosis of tuberculosis and other mycobacteria. At present mycobacterial culture relies on egg based Lowestin Jensen media or agar based Middle brook 7H10 or 7H11 and liquid medium such as Kirchner's or Middle brook 7H9 broth. The major constraint of culturing mycobacteria is its slow growth which necessitates its incubation for at least 4 weeks.

Others culture methods includes septi-check AFB method, Radiometric Bactec 460 TB method, MGIT 960 mycobacteria detection system, MB/ Bac T system, ESP culture system II and microscopic observation of broth culture.

Indirect Approach:-

Detection of antibodies for diagnosis of TB

Antibodies to mycobacterial antigens in sera of patients are detected either by using monoclonal or polyclonal antibodies. Cross reaction by environmental mycobacteria may produce false positive reactions. It is also important to note that the immune response in mycobacterial disease appears to be associated with HLA class II allotypes and different patients will recognize different antigens. Some of the newer approaches are TB STAT-PAK, Enzyme immuno assay for the detection of anti-mycobacterial suproxide dismutase antibody, Insta test TB, TB MPB 64 patch test, measurement of IFN gamma producing cells. (ICMR bulletin, 2002)

W H O Guidelines for Anti Tuberculosis Testing

In 1997 the World Health Organization (WHO), the International Union against Tuberculosis and Lung Disease (IUATLD) and partners world-wide released the first report of the global project on anti-tuberculosis drug resistance.

1) The data generated in this report were reinforced in a recently published second report.

2) Directly observed treatment short-course (DOTS), the WHO strategy for TB control cures virtually all patients with drug-susceptible TB and some drug resistant TB through the administration of short-course chemotherapy with first-line drugs.

3) However, patients with multidrug-resistant (MDR) tuberculosis (TB) to at least isoniazid and rifampicin are more likely to fail short-course chemotherapy. In recent years there has been encouraging evidence that patients with MDR TB can be cured with appropriate management based second-line drugs.

Unfortunately, second-line drugs are inherently more toxic and less effective than first-line drugs and reliable assessment of drug resistance is an essential prerequisite for appropriate use. Treatment is prolonged and significantly more expensive.

Accurate Laboratory drug susceptibility testing (DST) data to second-line drugs will support clinical decision making and help prevent the emergence of further drug resistance in patients with MDR TB. In order to meet the challenges posed by MDR TB, the WHO established the DOTS-Plus initiative to assess the feasibility and cost-effectiveness of using second-line drugs to manage patients with MDR TB primarily in middle and low-income countries. Reliable DST, including second-line drug testing, is a basic requirement of the DOTS-Plus strategy. Program officers and clinicians may not be aware that the intrinsic accuracy of susceptibility testing results (performed under the best circumstances) varies with the drug tested: it is most accurate for rifampicin and isoniazid and less for streptomycin and ethambutol. Data of comparable quality for classical second-line drugs are often fragmentary.

Second-line DST is unnecessary in first-line drug-susceptible cases. In the absence of drug resistance, first-line drugs are highly effective and second-line drugs should not be used except in the context of severe drug intolerance. To ensure accuracy of in-vitro susceptibility results for second-line drugs only laboratories with experience and well-documented competency in performing first-line drug testing should consider offering testing for second-line drugs. Consideration should be given to centralizing these analyses where appropriate. For example, a large body of clinical and bacteriological data exists for early trial drugs such as p-amino salicylic acid (PAS) but little exists for the use of fluoroquinolones and other new agents in the management of TB. In preparing the referred document the writing committee has tried to indicate the degree of evidence supporting our recommendations regarding appropriate methodologies for the analysis of second-line drug resistance.

Drug susceptibility of *M. tuberculosis* can be determined either by observation of growth or metabolic inhibition in a medium containing anti-tuberculosis drug, or by detection, at the molecular level, of mutations in the genes related to drug action. From a technical standpoint, drug susceptibility is determined on the basis of growth (or metabolic) inhibition induced by the drug by means of: 1) macroscopic observation of growth in drug-free and drug-containing media; 2) detection or measurement of the metabolic activity or products; 3) lysis with mycobacteriophage; and 4) detection of genetic mutations using molecular techniques.

Conventional culture methods using egg- or agar-based media are still the most utilized in many countries (Canetti G *et al.* 1969,Kent TK, Kubica GP,1985). Although the long turnaround time of DST results displeases physicians for the purpose of case management, it is suitable for DRS. The standard methods using Lowenstein–Jensen medium include the proportion method, the absolute concentration method and the resistant ratio method, which are fairly well standardized with clinical samples, at least for the major anti-tuberculosis drugs (Canetti G, *et al.* 1969). Among conventional methods, the proportion method is the most preferred choice, but the absolute concentration method is also commonly used on account of its technical simplicity for inoculum preparation and for reading the results.

In order to shorten the turnaround time and make it more convenient for case management, numerous new techniques have appeared, aiming to detect growth inhibition as early as possible. The most commonly used systems are detection of CO_2 production, such as BACTEC 460 (Hawkins JE,1991) or MB/Bact (Diaz-Infantes MS *et al.*1989) and oxygen consumption, such as *Mycobacterial* Growth Indicator Tube (Bemer P,*et.al*,2002). Other methods in developmental stage, include oxidation–reduction indicators like resazurin or tetrazolium bromide (Palomino JC,2002, Abate G,1998) and the phage-based techniques(Riska PF *et al.* 1999,Gali N, *et al.* 2003). Particle-counting immunoassay (Drowart A *et al.* 1997) can also curtail turnaround times by detecting a low-level multiplication of *M. tuberculosis.*

Many of those new techniques are difficult to implement in countries where they are needed the most, because of high costs, technical complexity and absence of appropriately trained human resources. In addition, they still need clinical evaluation to verify their claimed efficiency under various settings. Most of all, none of these techniques has been well calibrated with representative clinical samples of *M. tuberculosis* in order to determine the clinically relevant criteria of resistance (i.e. cut-off points). There are numerous reports on molecular techniques to detect gene mutations related to resistance, including hybridization (Lebrun L, *et al*, 2003,Van Der Zanden AG,*et al*,2003) of amplified gene segments or other PCR-based methods. However, not all resistance-related genes for the different anti-tuberculosis drugs and their sites of mutation have been found, except for *rpoB* gene mutations, which lead to Rifampicine resistance. These molecular techniques normally require primary amplification, and, therefore, when they are used on a routine basis for long periods of time, they are not free from false results due to contaminating amplicons and/or chromosomal DNA.

Treatment for Tuberculosis

The anti-tuberculosis agents were discovered during 1950s and 1960s. Streptomycin, p-aminosalicylic acid (1949), isoniazid (1952), pyrazinamide (1954), cycloserine(1955), ethambutol (1962), and rifampin (rifampicin;1963). (Anti-tubercle drugs [online]accessed on 18-05- 2014)

The drugs that have been used to fight tuberculosis include isoniazid, Rifampicine, Pyrazinamide, Ethambutol, Streptomycin, p-aminosalicylic acid, ethionamide, cycloserine, capremycine, kanamycine, thioacetazone etc. The first line drugs include Isoniazid, Rifampicin, Pyrazinamide, Streptomycin and Ethambutol.

Association of Tuberculosis infections with other disease

The co-infection of HIV and tuberculosis remain the major threat for patients. The HIV infected Tuberculosis patients are more difficult to manage as there is lower immune response as compared to that of patients having TB only. The two infections deteriorate the health of the patients and they suffer more from the treatment of tuberculosis. Globally about 30% of the HIV infected persons have the consistent latent infection of tuberculosis.

Indicators of hepato-cellular damages due to anti tuberculosis treatment

The aminotransferase (formerly transaminases) are the most frequently utilized and specific indicators of hepato-cellular necrosis. These enzymes- Aspartate aminotransferase (AST, formerly serum glutamate oxaloacetic transaminase-SGOT) and alanine amino-transferase (ALT, formerly serum glutamic pyruvate transaminase-SGPT) catalyze the transfer of the alpha-amino acids of aspartate and alanine respectively to the alpha-keto group of ketoglutaric acid. ALT is primarily localized to the liver but the AST is present in a wide variety of tissues like the heart, skeletal muscle, kidney, brain and liver.

Aspartate amino transferase (AST) catalyzes the interaction of alanine with alpha-ketoglutarate and results into oxaloacetate and glutamate.

Alanine amino transferase (ALT) catalyzes the interaction of alanine and alpha-ketoglutarate with resultant products pyruvate and glutamate.

Whereas the AST is present in both the mitochondria and cytosol of hepatocytes, ALT is localized to the cytosol. The cytosolic and mitochondrial forms of AST are true iso-enzymes and immunologically distinct.

Alkaline phosphatase

Alkaline phosphatase is a family of zinc metaloenzymes, with a serine at the active center; they release inorganic phosphate from various organic orthophosphates and are present in nearly all tissues. In liver, alkaline phosphatase is found histochemically in the microvilli of bile canaliculi and on the sinusoidal surface of hepatocytes. Alkaline phosphatase from the liver, bone and kidney are thought to be from the same gene but that from intestine and placenta are derived from different genes.

Serum Proteins and Albumins

The liver is the major source of most the serum proteins. The parenchymal cells are responsible for synthesis of albumin, fibrinogen and other coagulation factors and most of the alpha and beta globulins. Albumin: Albumin is quantitatively the most important protein in plasma synthesized by the liver and is a useful indicator of hepatic function. Because the half life of albumin in serum is as long as 20 days, the serum albumin level is not a reliable indicator of hepatic protein synthesis in acute liver disease. Albumin synthesis is affected not only in liver disease but also by nutritional status, hormonal balance and osmotic pressure. Liver is the only site of synthesis of albumin. The serum levels are typically depressed in patients with cirrhosis and ascites. In patients with or without ascites, the serum albumin level correlates with prognosis. Normal serum values range from 3.5g/dl to 4.5 g/dl. The average adult has approximately 300 to 500 g of albumin. The serum levels at any time reflect its rate of synthesis, degradation and volume of distribution.

The serum protein level assessment is an indicator of the hepato-cellular damages due to side effects of anti tubercle medicine intake. The determination of serum proteins is useful for assaying the degree of activity of tuberculosis lesion (Jorge A. Pilheu *et.al.*,1962).

The region-wise and blood group wise studies were performed for the prevalence of tuberculosis infection. The study done by the researchers confirmed that the some blood group in given area is more prone for infection than other.

Use of herbs for tuberculosis treatment

The side effects of the anti tubercle drugs and long course of treatment are two big problems in eradication of the disease. The indigenous herbs of medicinal importance may serve to be a better option over the traditional medicines for tuberculosis. The traditional practice of herbal drugs comprise medicinal plants, minerals, and organic matter; etc. Herbal drugs constitute only those traditional medicines, which primarily use plant preparations for therapy. The earliest recorded evidence of their use in Indians, Chinese, Egyptian, Greek, Roman and Syrian texts dates back to about 5000 years. The classical Indian texts include Rig-Veda, Ayurveda, Charak Samhita and Sushruta Samhita. The herbal/traditional medicine had been devised from rich traditions of ancient civilization and scientific heritage. (Kamboj V.P.*et.al.*., 2000) Plant based active principles can be derived from bark, leaves, flowers, roots, fruits, seeds, and the others. (Gorden MC *et.al.*.,2001)

Some plants also available in India are already tested for the anti tubercle action by incorporation of the extracts in Lowenstein Jensen medium (Renu Gupta *et al*, 2010). These plants are as under:-

01 *Acalypha indica L.(Euphorbiaceae)*

02 *Adhatoda vasica Nees.(Acanthaceae)*

03 *Allium cepa L (Alliaceae)*

04 *Allium sativum (Alliaceae)*

05 *Aloe vera L* .(Aloaceae)

In the present study certain plants, which reportedly have significant anti-microbial / anti - tubercular effect in traditional usage, were screened *in vitro* for their anti-tubercular activity against *Mycobacterium tuberculosis.* These are namely, *Abutilon indicum* (Family:-Malvacea) commonly known as Chakrabhenda, which is common throughout the hotter parts of India., *Allium cepa,* (Family:- Liliacea) commonly known as onion extensively cultivated all over the India., *Andrographis peniculata* (Family:- Acanthaceae) commonly known as chiretta, an erect annual herb found in semi evergreen forest of India., *Pheonix dactylifera* (Family:-Palmea) commonly known as Khajur or Date palm in many parts of India (Joshi S. G. *et al.*2000). The objectives of the study include the evaluation of the degree of side effects of the anti tubercle treatment on Liver by various tests like serum ALT, serum AST, serum ALP, Total Proteins and albumins, A/G Ratio of the tuberculosis patients of different categories of treatment like Catgory I, II, and III and also TB+HIV cases. The blood of the tuberculosis patients also surveyed for the blood grouping analysis for finding any specific blood group to be more prone for tubercle infections over the others.

The anti tubercle action of the herbal extracts and highlight the adverse side effects of the routine drugs presently used to combat the tuberculosis the following tasks were undertaken. Collection, identification and authentication of plant species, Processing and extraction of plant materials , correlate and compare the anti-tubercle activity between routine medicine and isolated plant extracts, correlate blood groups and its relation with tuberculosis, study the relation between vitamin C and anti TB action of the plant extracts used, Estimation of common serum enzymes observed in TB patients with routine chemotherapy of TB, Comparative study of protein, albumin and protein / albumin ratio in normal person, TB patient and TB+HIV patients and the Stastical Analysis of the data obtained to reach the conclusion.

Taxonomic classification of Mycobacterium tuberculosis:-

Kingdom	*Bacteria*
Phylum	*Actinobacteria*
Class	*Actinobacteria*
Order	*Actinomycetales*
Suborder	*Corynebacterineae*
Family	*Mycobacteriaceae*
Genus	*Mycobacterium*
Species	*M. tuberculosis*
Binomial name	*Mycobacterium tuberculosis*
Synonyms	*Tubercle bacillus* Koch 1882

(http://en.wikipedia.org/wiki/Mycobacterium_tuberculosis[online],accessed on14-05-2014)

CHAPTER THREE

Review of Tuberculosis

Consumption, Phthisis, Scrofula, Pott's disease, and the White Plague are all terms used to refer to tuberculosis throughout history. This was focused attention of killer disease from ancient times around over the world. The human being tried to fight with the disease and discovered tools and techniques for combating the disease and to overcome the problem.

In early 17th century there was an epidemic in Europe which affected almost 200 years and peoples of that area known it as the Great White Plague. In 1650 tuberculosis was considered inevitable, being the principal cause of death.(History of tuberculosis [online] accessed on 31-05-2014)

The most convincing case was found in the mummy of priest Nesperehen, discovered by Grebart in 1881, which featured evidence of spinal tuberculosis with the characteristic psoas abscesses.Similar features were discovered on other mummies like that of the priest Philoc and throughout the cemeteries of Thebes. Evidence of the disease found in Egyptian mummies dated between 3000 and 2400 BC which are recorded in 2008. The Neolithic mummies were approximate 9000 years old. Some authors call tuberculosis the first disease known to mankind. (History of tuberculosis [online] accessed on 31-05-2014)

The first references to tuberculosis in Asian civilization are found in the Vedas. The oldest of them (Rigveda, 1500 BC) calls the disease *yaksma*. The Atharvaveda calls it another name: *balasa*. It is in the Atharvaveda that the first description of scrofula is given. The *Sushruta Samhita*, written around 600 BC, recommends that the disease be treated with breast milk, various meats, alcohol and rest. The Yajurveda advises sufferers to move to higher altitudes. (Kenneth G. Zysk 1998)

In South America, the first evidence of the disease is found in the Arawak culture around 1050 BC, although the most significant finding belongs to the mummy of an 8 to 10-year-old Nascan child from Hacienda Agua Sala, dated to 700 AD. Scientists were able to isolate evidence of the bacillus.

In the year 1854, Hermann Brehmer a Silesian botanist in his doctoral dissertation entitled Tuberculosis is a Curable Disease. His theories were based on his own experience in which he had the disease and moved to the Himalayas. While there to study botany, he was cured of the disease.

After that, Robert Koch created a stain that identifies the disease in 1882 which allows biologists to fight against it more accurately. The statement made by Robert Koch became the benchmark in the discoveries towards the treatment of tuberculosis and combating against the tuberculosis. The statement was "I have no business to live this life if I cannot eradicate this horrible scourge from the mankind," Robert Koch, delivering a lecture at Berlin University on his discovery of tuberculosis bacilli, 1882(drug regimen for tb,[online]accesses on 24-05-2014).

M. tuberculosis, then known as the "tubercle bacillus" and the bacterium is also known as "Koch's bacillus"

M. tuberculosis has an unusual, waxy coating on its cell surface (primarily mycolic acid, which makes the cells impervious to Gram staining.Acid-fast detection techniques are used instead. The physiology of *M. tuberculosis* is highly aerobic and requires high levels of oxygen. Primarily a pathogen of the mammalian respiratory system, MTB (*Mycobacterium tuberculosis*) infects the lungs. The most frequently used diagnostic methods for TB are the tuberculin skin test, acid-fast stain, and chest radiographs. After Koch's discovery, many attempts were made over the years to find a compound that could stop the growth of TB bacteria. In 1910, a German scientist named Paul Ehrlich discovered a chemical that could kill the microorganism that causes another disease, syphilis, and effectively treat that disease. This initiated the search for other chemical substances which could destroy disease-causing microorganisms.

In 1935, a German scientist Gerhard Domagk published a report on the use of "Prontosil," an organic compound containing sulfur (sulfanilamide), for treatment of bacterial infections. Domagk was awarded The Nobel Prize in Physiology or Medicine for his discovery in 1939. Prontosil, and derivatives of it, had some effect on TB bacteria in laboratory studies, but only in concentrations that would be poisonous to humans (Hager Thomas,2006).

Unfortunately, early in the studies, it became evident that the TB bacteria were becoming resistant to streptomycin. This severely reduced the usefulness of the drug for treating tuberculosis.

Year 1943 begins with the discovery of new drug called para-aminosalicylic acid (PAS). This drug was used in combination with streptomycin to prevent TB bacteria from becoming resistant. However, the patient had to use the drugs for periods of months in order to be cured. Another drug called "isoniazid," a derivative of a compound researched earlier by Domagk, was developed in 1952.

Thus, in the decade between 1944 and 1954, largely due to the work of Nobel Laureates, three drugs - streptomycin, PAS and isoniazid – became available. When taken in combination, and for a sufficient length of time, the prognosis for a patient with TB disease changed from dismal to the expectation of cure.

Today, the cornerstone for any treatment of tuberculosis is still multi-drug therapy. At least two drugs are given at the same time to prevent the emergence of drug resistance. Sometimes patients are treated with up to four different antibacterial drugs, and for periods of a minimum of 6 to 24 months.

Indian Scenario of tuberculosis

Despite the courageous efforts of Koch and his successors, TB has not yet been eliminated and is especially prevalent in poor and developing countries. Tuberculosis threatens the health of millions in our country. With 1.8 million cases occurring annually, India accounts for a fifth of the world's new TB cases and $2/3^{rd}$ of the cases in South-East Asia. This makes India the highest TB burden country in the world. It has been estimated for the year 2000, that there were about 3.8 million bacteriological positive TB cases in the country. In view of the side effects of the present anti tubercle medicinal usage there are many side effects and the side effects are making hurdle towards obtaining a 100% cure rate in tuberculosis patients. The side effects can be assessed by various indicators like pain and inflammation felt by the patients on anti-tubercle treatment and assessing the liver function tests (LFT) as the anti-tubercle drugs mainly damages the Liver. (Simpson DG, Walker JH 1960)

In 1908, two Frenchmen, Calmette and Guerin, began to develop a vaccine for tuberculosis by passaging *M. bovis* 230 times. By 1921 they believed they had developed a vaccine of sufficient attenuation to provide a safe protection (White A *et al.*2013).

To control and prevent the tuberculosis (TB), India started their research since the start of the 20th century and in 1906 through a Christian organization, and the first open-air sanatorium was established in Tilounia, at Ajmer, Rajasthan. Later on additional sanatoria, dispensaries and societies were established throughout the country. In 1929, India joined the International Union Against Tuberculosis (IUAT) and the King George V Thanks giving Fund for TB control was established and administered through central, state and provincial committees to support TB education and prevention, establish clinics, and train health workers. The TB Association of India (TAI) was established in 1939, to develop standard methods for managing TB and to develop model training institutions. In 1946, the committee outlined a plan for the management of the estimated 2.5 million TB patients with a TB clinic in every district and mobile clinics in rural areas. After independence in 1949, the Central Government of Independent India established a TB Division within the Directorate General of Health Services of the Ministry of Health to oversee the plan. Over the next 20 years, new TB drugs became available: streptomycin in 1944; PAS in 1946; thiacetazone in 1950; isoniazid in 1952; and rifampicin in 1966.

In 1959 the Government of India, with the help of World Health Organization (W.H.O), established the National TB Institute (NTI) in Bangalore to develop a National TB control programme (NTP), with the aim of establishing prompt diagnosis and ambulatory treatment which were integrated into general health services. (National TB Institute [online] accessed on 31-05-2014)

After independence with continuous efforts taken by various National and international Organizations by 2006, the whole country was covered under the RNTCP, and case detection and treatment success rates had improved significantly. The challenge is now to sustain the existing DOTS-based programme while introducing all components of the new Stop TB strategy, including services to address TB/HIV, treatment for multidrug-resistant TB, strengthening laboratory services, and integrating TB services in all health facilities of both the public and private health-care sectors. Over the next few years, routine notification data supplemented by prevalence surveys may be used to determine the impact of TB control. India is in a position to achieve the Millennium Development Goal (MDG) and Stop TB Partnership targets by 2015 but this will require increases in funding and human resources, more intensive engagement with all health-care providers and strengthened regulation of anti-TB drugs.(RNTCP History [online]accessed on 31-05-2014)

Karyadi, E., C.E. West, W. Schultink, *et al.* (2000) reported that the serum zinc, calcium and albumin zinc levels were significantly low among tuberculosis patients as compared to healthy control. The possible causes for low serum zinc and albumin in pulmonary tuberculosis patients were considered to be nutritional factors, enteropathy and acute phase reactant proteins. The hepatic synthesis of acute phase reactant proteins is induced by cytokines such as interleukin-6 and tumor necrosis factor (Xing, Z., J. *et al.* 1998), which inhibit the production of serum albumin and cause dramatic shift in the plasma concentration of certain essential micronutrients and albumin.

Prevalence of tuberculosis in various blood groups

The region-wise and blood groups wise studies were performed as survey study for the prevalence of tuberculosis infection. The study done by the researchers confirmed that the some blood group in given area is more prone for infection then other.

A human blood group chimera was illustrated by Saha *et al.* (1968) described incidence of ABO and Rh Blood groups in Pulmonary Tuberculosis in different ethenic Groups. Tyagi *et al.* (1967) explored that blood genetics in pulmonary tuberculosis referred the pioneer work of Aird *et al.* (1953) many workers have tried to correlate the susceptibility of various diseases in relation to blood groups (Aird *et al.* 1954. Tyagi *et al.* 1965, 1966). The incidence of ABO blood groups in pulmonary tuberculosis have been reviewed by different many researchers (Jain 1970 and Thamaria *et al.* 1972), the differences in results obtained by those researchers initiates a study to assess any genetic relationship of ABO and Rhesus blood groups and secretion of blood group specific substances in saliva in cases of pulmonary tuberculosis. As a result they found out of 580 cases of pulmonary tuberculosis 23.10% were of group A, 43.45% of group B, 27.59% of group O and 5.86% of group AB. Amongst control cases 24.69% were of group A, 35.25% of group B, 31.29% of group O and 8.77% of group AB. The incidence of Rhesus negative was 3.27% in cases of pulmonary tuberculosis and 3.4% in control series. They found in their reports in the literature have shown a great variation in the frequency of ABO blood groups in pulmonary tuberculosis. Nath *et al.* 1963 reported a high prevalence of group O in pulmonary tuberculosis. Thamaria *et al.* (1972) while studying the ABO frequency in 118 bacillary pulmonary tuberculosis cases reported a high prevalence of group O. Thamaria *et.al* (1972) describe the frequency distribution of ABO blood groups among general population of Northern Rajasthan and among sputum positive pulmonary tuberculosis case with particular reference to rate of in-activation of isoniazid.

Recently, Rao *et al.* (2012) described the ABO group distribution and pulmonary tuberculosis and found that a significant association was observed between the incidence of tuberculosis and the blood groups B and AB (P values are 0.048 and 0.03 respectively). The association between the incidence of tuberculosis and the blood groups A and O (P values are 0.249 and 0.069 respectively) was found insignificant. However, a significant association between the incidence of tuberculosis and a positive Rhesus antigen was observed in the blood group A (P value is 0.009). But there was no significant association between the incidence of tuberculosis and a positive Rhesus antigen with the blood groups B, AB and O and study showed that there was an association between tuberculosis and the blood groups B and AB in this region of the Andhra Pradesh state

Treatment for tuberculosis

Treatment for tuberculosis (TB) depends on the type of tuberculosis, although a long course of antibiotics is most often used. While TB is a serious condition that can be fatal if left untreated, deaths are rare if treatment is completed. For most people, hospital admission during treatment is not necessary.

If diagnosed with active pulmonary TB (TB that affects the lungs and causes symptoms), patient will be referred to a specialist TB treatment team.

Side effects of treatment for tuberculosis: The antibiotics used to treat TB can cause damage to the liver or the eyes. Rifampicin can reduce the effectiveness of some types of contraception, such as the combined contraceptive pill.

Antibiotic-resistant tuberculosis (TB): Like most bacteria, bacteria that cause TB can develop a resistance to antibiotics. This means the medicines can no longer kill the bacteria they are meant to fight. Tuberculosis (TB) that develops a resistance to one type of antibiotic is not usually a concern because alternative antibiotics are available. In 2011, more than eight out of 100 cases of TB were resistant to at least one type of antibiotic normally used to treat the condition. (Antibiotic resistant tb[online]accessed on 31-05-2014)

However, in a number of cases: TB develops a resistance to two antibiotics – this is known as multi-drug resistant tuberculosis (MDR-TB)

TB develops a resistance to three or more antibiotics – this is known as extensively drug resistant tuberculosis (XDR-TB)

Multi drug-resistant tuberculosis (MDR-TB) caused by *Mycobacterium tuberculosis,* which is resistant to both Isoniazide and Rifampicin with or without resistance to other drugs. Globally, about three per cent of all newly diagnosed patients have MDR-TB. The proportion is higher in patients who have previously received anti-tuberculosis treatment reflecting the failure of programmes designed to ensure complete cure of patients with tuberculosis. While host genetic factors may probably contribute, incomplete and inadequate treatment is the most important factor leading to the development of MDR-TB. The definitive diagnosis of MDR-TB is difficult in resource poor low income countries because of non-availability of reliable laboratory facilities. Efficiently run tuberculosis control programmes based on directly observed treatment, short-course (DOTS) policy is essential for preventing the emergence of MDR-TB. Management of MDR-TB is a challenge which should be undertaken by experienced clinicians at centers equipped with reliable laboratory service for mycobacterial culture and *in vitro* sensitivity testing as it requires prolonged use of expensive second-line drugs with a significant potential for toxicity. Judicious use of drugs, supervised individualized treatment, focused clinical, radiological and bacteriological follow up, use of surgery at the appropriate juncture are key factors in the successful management of these patients. In certain areas, currently available programme approach may not be adequate and innovative approaches such as DOTS-plus may have to be employed to effectively control MDR-TB. The emergence of drug resistance in *M.tuberculosis* has been associated with a variety of management, health provider and patient-related factors. These include

(i) Deficient or deteriorating TB control programmes resulting in inadequate administration of effective treatment;

(ii) Poor case holding, administration of sub-standard drugs, inadequate or irregular drug supply and lack of supervision;

(iii) Ignorance of health care workers in epidemiology, treatment and control;

(iv) Improper prescription of regimens;

(v) Interruption of chemotherapy due to side effects;

(vi) Non-adherence of patients to the prescribed drug therapy;

(vii) Availability of anti-TB drugs across the counter, without prescription;

(viii) Massive bacillary load;

(ix) Illiteracy and low socio-economic status of the patients;

(x) The epidemic of HIV infection;

(xi) Laboratory delays in identification and susceptibility testing of M. tuberculosis isolates;

(xii) Use of non standardized laboratory techniques, poor quality drug powders and lack of quality control measures; and

(xiii) Use of anti-TB drugs for indications other than tuberculosis.

Mechanism and transmission of drug resistance:-

Drug resistance in *Mycobacterium tuberculosis* occurs by random, single step, spontaneous mutation at a low but predictable frequency, in large bacterial populations. The probability of incidence of drug resistant mutants is for rifampicin, while for isoniazid and some of the other commonly used drugs. (Guidelines for surveillance of drug resistance in tuberculosis, WHO/TB/96.216. 1997, Paramasivan CN,1998)

Therefore, the probability for resistance to both isoniazid and rifampicin to develop is much larger than the number of organisms present in a medium sized cavity in a patient with open pulmonary TB. (Devaki V, *et al.* 1969)

For several years, drug resistant strains of *M. tuberculosis* were considered to be less infectious than the drug susceptible ones, recent studies have demonstrated that the drug resistant mutants are equally infectious and can cause severe disease in an individual exposed to the same. (Snider DE Jr, *et al.* 1985)

Detection of drug resistance

The conventional methods of culture, identification and drug susceptibility testing of the isolated organism require a minimum of 10-12 week. Although most widely used, the long waiting period in obtaining the results by these methods may delay the initiation of proper treatment, resulting in the patient transmitting drug-resistant infection in the community. The use of direct sensitivity tests, especially to isoniazid and rifampicin has resulted in a saving of at least 4 week in obtaining the resistance status (Mathew S, *et al.* 1995). However, this method is not very useful in smear-negative and paucibacillary specimens. Several newer methods including molecular diagnostics have resulted in cutting down the time interval between collection of the specimen and the receipt of results to 2-3 week or even less. On the other hand, these methods require considerable technical expertise and impose financial constraints in a routine laboratory set up in the developing nations (Paramasivan C.N., *et al.* 2004).

Table No. 02:- showing treatment Regimen in DOTs

Category of treatment	Type of patient	Regimen*
Category I	New sputum smear-positive Seriously ill** new sputum smear-negative Seriously ill** new extra-pulmonary	2H3R3Z3E3+ 4H3R3
Category II	Sputum smear-positive Relapse Sputum smear-positive Failure Sputum smear-positive Treatment After Default, Others***	2H3R3Z3E3S3+ 1H3R3Z3E3+ 5H3R3E3
Category III	New Sputum smear-negative, not seriously ill New Extra-pulmonary, not seriously ill	2H3R3Z3+ 4H3R3

*The number before the letters refers to the number of months of treatment.

The subscript after the letters refers to the number of doses per week. The dosage strengths are as follows: H: Isoniazid (600 mg), R: Rifampicin (450 mg), Z: Pyrazinamide (1500 mg), E: Ethambutol (1200 mg), S: Streptomycin (750 mg).

Streptomycin

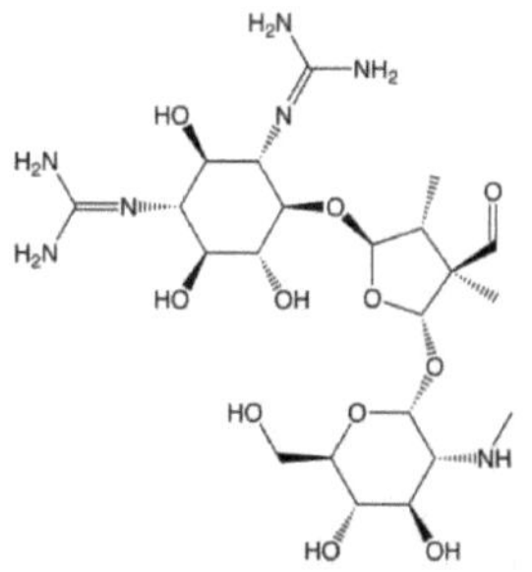

Chemical structure of streptomycin

Streptomycin was first discovered by Albert Schatz, in the year 1943 (Comroe JH Jr, 1978). In Selman Waksman's laboratory, streptomycin was the first drug used successfully to treat tuberculosis. This is a protein synthesis inhibitor (REF). Streptomycin is an antibiotic (anti-mycobacterial) drug, the first of a class of drugs called amino-glycosides, and it was the first antibiotic remedy for tuberculosis. It is derived from the actinobacterium *Streptomyces griseus*. Streptomycin is a bactericidal antibiotic. Adverse effects of this medicine are ototoxicity, nephrotoxicity, fetal auditory toxicity, and neuromuscular paralysis. Streptomycin was the first antibiotic that could be used to cure the disease tuberculosis (TB) (streptomycin [online] accessed on 18-05-2014)

Pharmacokinetics

Streptomycin is a protein synthesis inhibitor. It binds to the small 16S rRNA of the 30S subunit of the bacterial ribosome, interfering with the binding of formyl-methionyl-tRNA to the 30S subunit (Sharma D, 2007). This leads to codon misreading, eventual inhibition of protein synthesis and ultimately death of microbial cells through mechanisms that are still not understood. Speculation on this mechanism indicates that the binding of the molecule to the 30S subunit interferes with 50S subunit association with the mRNA strand. This results in an unstable ribosomal-mRNA complex, leading to a frame shift mutation and defective protein synthesis; leading to cell death. Humans have structurally different ribosome from bacteria, thereby allowing the selectivity of this antibiotic for bacteria. At low concentrations, however, Streptomycin only inhibits growth of the bacteria by inducing prokaryotic ribosome to misread mRNA (Voet, Donald & Voet,2004). Streptomycin is an antibiotic that inhibits both Gram-positive and Gram-negative bacteria, and is therefore a useful broad-spectrum antibiotic.

Rifampicin

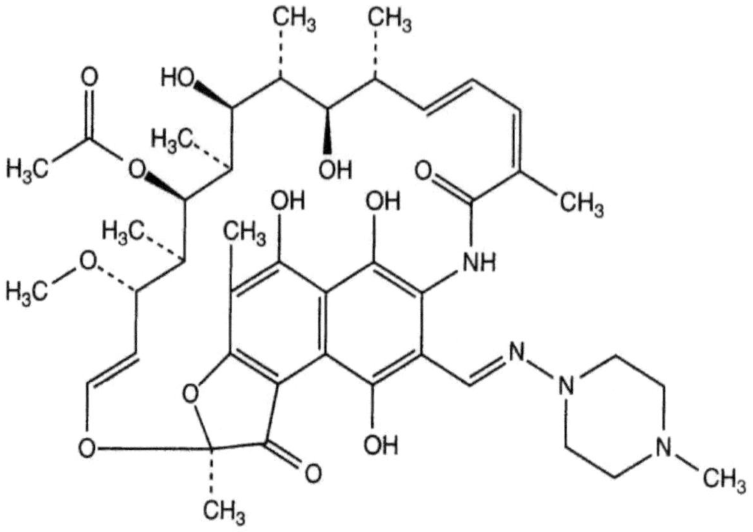

Chemical structure of Rifampicin

Rifampicin is a bactericidal antibiotic drug of the rifamycin group. Rifampicin is also used as an anti-mycobacterial: it acts by interfering with the DNA-dependent RNA polymerase of bacterial cells. The action of rifampicin prevents production of messenger RNA and thus ultimately stops protein.

In 1957, a soil sample from a pine forest on the French Riviera was brought for analysis to the Lepetit Pharmaceuticals research lab in Milan, Italy. A research group headed by Prof. Piero Sensi (1920-2013) and Dr. Maria Teresa Timbal (1925 - 1969) discovered a new bacterium. This new species was producing a new class of molecules with antibiotic activity. Because Sensi, Timbal and the researchers were particularly fond of the French crime story *Rififi* they call these compounds as "rifamycins". After two years of attempts to obtain more stable semi-synthetic products, a new molecule with high efficacy and good tolerability was produced in 1959 and was named "rifampicin" .(Rifampicine[online]accessed on 31-05-2014)

Rifampicin is also known as rifaldazine, RMP, rofact (in Canada), and rifampin in the United States. There are various types of rifamycins from which this is derived, but the rifampicin form, with a 4-methyl-1-piperazinaminyl group, is by far the most clinically effective.

Rifampicin is an intensely red solid, and the small fraction which reaches body fluids is known for imparting a harmless red-orange colour to the urine (and to a lesser extent, also sweat and tears) of users, for a few hours after a dose. Maximal concentrations in the blood are decreased by about a third when the antibiotic is taken with food.

Rifampicin was introduced in 1967, as a major addition to the cocktail-drug treatment of tuberculosis and inactive meningitis, along with pyrazinamide, isoniazid, ethambutol, and streptomycin ("PIERS") It requires a prescription in North America. It must be administered regularly daily for several months without break; otherwise, the risk of drug-resistant tuberculosis is greatly increased (Long, James W.1991). In fact, this is the primary reason it is used in tandem with the three aforementioned drugs, particularly isoniazid. This is also the primary motivation behind directly observed therapy for tuberculosis (Erlich, Henry *et al.* 1973).

Rifampicin resistance develops quickly during treatment, so monotherapy should not be used to treat these infections — it should be used in combination with other antibiotics.

Rifampicin is also used in the treatment of cholestatic pruritus. Rifampicin is typically used to treat *Mycobacterium* infections, including tuberculosis and leprosy (Hansen's disease). It can be used to treat abscesses, as an uncommon complication of BCG vaccination for tuberculosis. There is no difference between a three to four month regimen of rifampicin and a six to nine month regimen for preventing active tuberculosis in those with

HIV-negative latent tuberculosis. The quality of the evidence was however low (Sharma, SK; *et al.*2013). With multidrug therapy used as the standard treatment of Hansen's disease, rifampicin is always used in combination with dapsone and clofazimine to avoid eliciting drug resistance. Rifampicin is also used in the treatment of methicillin-resistant *Staphylococcus aureus* (MRSA) in combination with fusidic acid, including in difficult to treat infections such as osteomyelitis and prosthetic joint infections (Aboltins CA *et al.* 2007). It is also used in prophylactic therapy against *Neisseria meningitidis* (meningococcal) infection. Rifampicin is also recommended as an alternative treatment for infections with the tick-borne disease pathogens, *Borrelia burgdorferi* and *Anaplasma phagocytophilum* when treatment with doxycycline is contraindicated, such as in pregnant women or in patients with a history of allergy to tetracycline antibiotics (Wormser *et al.*2006 and Thomas RG *et al.*2009). It is also used to treat infections by *Listeria* species, *Neisseria gonorrhoeae*, *Haemophilus influenzae*, and *Legionella pneumophila*. For these nonstandard indications, sensitivity testing should be done (if possible) before starting rifampicin therapy. The Enterobacteriaceae and *Acinetobacter* and *Pseudomonas* species are intrinsically resistant to rifampicin. Further, it has been used with amphotericin B in largely unsuccessful attempts to treat primary amoebic meningoencephalitis caused by *Naegleria fowleri*. Rifampicin can be used as monotherapy for a few days as prophylaxis against meningitis, but resistance develops quickly during long treatment of active infections, so the drug is always used against active infections in combination with other antibiotics. Rifampicin has some effectiveness against vaccinia virus (Sodeik B *et al.* 1994 and Charity JC *et al.* 2007). The most serious adverse effect is related to rifampicin's hepatotoxicity, and patients receiving it often undergo baseline and frequent liver function tests to detect liver damage. As a consequence, rifampicin can cause a range of adverse reactions when taken concurrently with other drugs. For instance, patients undergoing long term anticoagulation therapy with warfarin have to be especially cautious and increase their dosage of warfarin accordingly. Failure to do so could lead to under-treating with anticoagulation, resulting in serious consequences of thromboembolism. Up-regulation of hepatic metabolism of hormones decreases their levels, and rifampicin can also in similar fashion reduce the efficacy of hormonal contraception, to the extent the unintended pregnancies have been reported among users of oral contraceptives taking rifampicin in even short courses (for example, as prophylaxis against exposure to bacterial meningitis). The more common unwanted effects include fever, gastrointestinal disturbances, rashes, and immunological reactions (G Curci *et al.*1969) Taking rifampicin can cause certain bodily fluids, such as urine and tears, to become orange-red in colour, a benign side effect which can be frightening if it is not expected and prepared for. This effect may also be used to monitor effective absorption of the drug (if drug colour is not seen in the urine, the patient may wish to move the drug dose farther in time from food or milk intake). The discolorizion of sweat and tears is not directly noticeable, but sweat may stain light clothing orange, and tears may permanently stain soft contact lenses. Since rifampicin may be excreted in breast milk, breast feeding should be avoided while it is being taken.

Adverse effects include:

- Hepatotoxic - hepatitis, liver failure in severe cases
- Respiratory - breathlessness
- Cutaneous - flushing, pruritus, rash, redness and watering of eyes
- Abdominal - nausea, vomiting, abdominal cramps with or without diarrhea
- Flu-like symptoms - with chills, fever, headache, arthralgia, and malaise, rifampin has good penetration into the brain, and this may directly explain some malaise and dysphoria in a minority of users (Stockley,Ivan H 1994)

When the rifampicin orally administered results in peak plasma concentrations in about 2 to 4 hours. 4-Aminosalicylic acid (another anti-tuberculosis drug) significantly reduces absorption of rifampicin and peak concentrations may not be reached. If these two drugs must be used concurrently (which happens often in treatment of TB), they must be given separately with an interval of eight to 12 hours between administrations (Curci G, *et al.* 1969)

Rifampicin is easily absorbed from the gastrointestinal tract; its ester functional group is quickly hydrolyzed in the bile; and it is catalyzed by a high pH and substrate-specific enzymes called esterase. After about 6 hours, almost the entire drug is deacetylated. Even in this deacetylated form, rifampin is still a potent antibiotic. Though, it can no longer be reabsorbed by the intestines and it is subsequently eliminated from the body.

The half-life of rifampicin ranges from 1.5 to 5.0 hours, though hepatic impairment will significantly increase it. Food consumption, on the other hand, inhibits absorption from the Gastrointestinal (GI) tract, and the drug is more quickly eliminated. When rifampicin is taken with a meal, peak blood concentration falls by 36%. Antacids do not affect absorption; however, the decrease in rifampin absorption with food is sometimes enough to noticeably affect urine color, which can be used as a marker for whether or not a dose of the drug has been effectively absorbed. (Hofmann, AF 2002)

Isoniazid

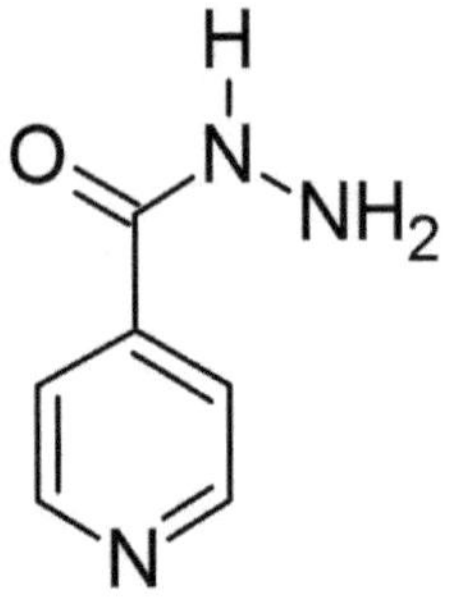

H
N
O
NH2
N

Chemical Structure of Isoniazide

The anti-mycobacterial drug isoniazid inhibits the formation of very long chain fatty acids such as those found in the cell walls of mycobacteria. Isoniazid is used in the treatment of tuberculosis and other mycobacterial infections.

Isoniazid (Laniazid, Nydrazid), is also known as isonicotinylhydrazine (INH), it is an organic compound that is the first-line medication in the treatment of tuberculosis. The compound was first synthesized in the early 20th century, but its activity against tuberculosis was first reported in the early 1950s, and three pharmaceutical companies attempted unsuccessfully to simultaneously patent the drug, (Hans L Riede 2009) the most prominent one being Roche, which launched its version, Rimifon, in 1952. Isoniazid is available in tablet, syrup, and injectable forms (given intramuscularly or intravenously). It is available worldwide, is inexpensive and is generally well tolerated. It is manufactured from isonicotinic acid, which is produced from 4-methylpyridine.

Side effects

Adverse reactions include rash, abnormal liver function tests, hepatitis, sideroblastic anemia, high anion gap metabolic acidosis, peripheral neuropathy, mild central nervous system (CNS) effects, drug interactions resulting in increased phenytoin (Dilantin) or disulfiram (Antabuse) levels, intractable seizures (status epilepticus) and drug-induced lupus erythematosus. (Isoniazide [online] accessed on 31-05-2014)

Peripheral neuropathy and CNS effects are associated with the use of isoniazid and are due to pyridoxine (vitamin B6) depletion, but are uncommon at doses of 5 mg/kg.

Hepatotoxicity of INH is by nitrogen group in its chemical structure, as it is metabolized in the liver and gets converted to an ammonium molecule, which causes hepatitis.

Hepatotoxicity can be avoided with close clinical monitoring of the patient, to be specific, nausea, vomiting, abdominal pain, and appetite. Isoniazid is metabolized by the liver mainly by acetylation and dehydrazination. The N-acetylhydrazine metabolite is believed to be responsible for the hepatotoxic effects seen in patients treated with isoniazid. The rate of acetylation is genetically determined. Approximately 50% of blacks and Caucasians are slow inactivators; the majority of Inuit and Asians are rapid inactivators. The half-life in fast acetylators is one to two hours, while in slow acetylators; it is two to five hours. Elimination is largely independent of renal function, but the half-life may be prolonged in liver disease.

The rate of acetylation has not been shown to significantly alter the effectiveness of isoniazid. However, slow acetylation may lead to higher blood concentrations with chronic administration of the drug, with an increased risk of toxicity. Fast acetylation leads to higher blood levels of the toxic metabolite acetylisoniazid and thus to an increase in toxic reactions - hepatitis which is 250 times more common than in slow acetylators. Isoniazid and its metabolites are excreted in the urine with 75 to 95% of the dose excreted in 24 hours. Small amounts are also excreted in saliva, sputum, and feces. Isoniazid is removed by haemodialysis and peritoneal dialysis(Frontali C., *et al.* 1965).

Headache, poor concentration, weight gain, poor memory, insomnia and depression have all been associated with isoniazid use. All patients and healthcare workers should be aware of these serious adverse effects, especially if suicidal thinking or behavior are suspected (Collins, R Douglas, 1985, Campbell, E.A., *et al.* 2001, Feklistov, A, *et al.* 2008,).

As previously mentioned, isoniazid is associated with pyridoxine deficiency. Pyridoxyl phosphate (derivative of pyridoxine, i.e. Vitamin B6) is required for d-aminolevulinic acid synthase, the enzyme responsible for the rate-limiting step in heme synthesis. As such, isoniazid-induced pyridoxine-deficiency leads to insufficient heme formation in early red blood cells, leading to sideroblastic anaemia (Girling DJ,1978).

Ethambutol

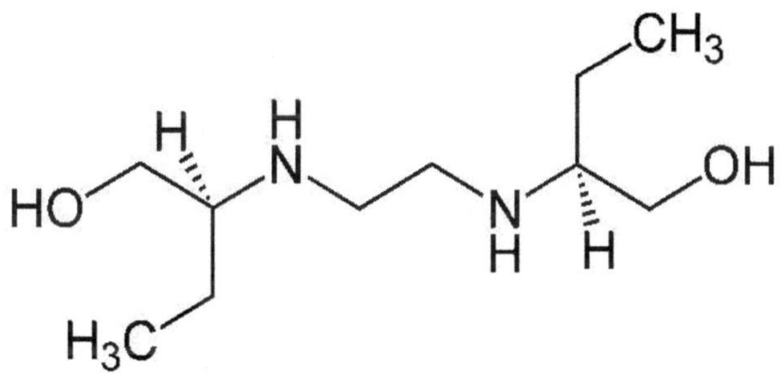

Chemical structure of Ethambutol

Ethambutol is a first-line anti-mycobacterial drug that inhibits cell wall synthesis although its mode of action remains to be elucidated fully. Ethambutol (commonly abbreviated EMB or simply E) is a bacteriostatic anti-mycobacterial drug prescribed to treat tuberculosis. It is usually given in combination with other tuberculosis drugs, such as isoniazid, rifampicin and pyrazinamide.

The adverse effects of Ethambutol includes the Optic neuritis (hence contraindicated in children below six years of age), Red-green colour blindness, Peripheral neuropathy, Arthralgia, Hepatotoxicity, Hyperuricemia, Vertical nystagmus, Milk skin reaction(ATS doc,2006).

Pyrazinamide

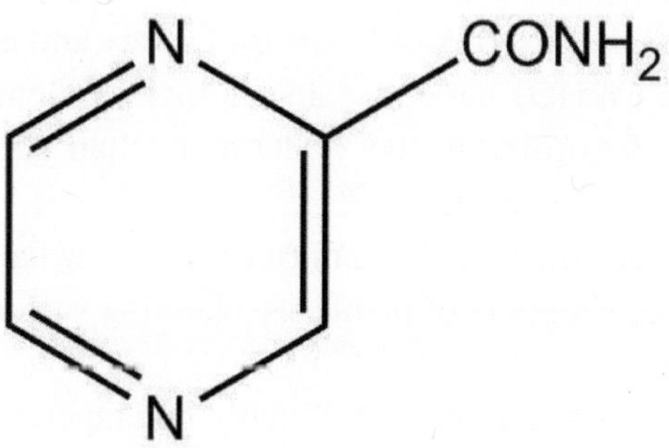

Chemical structure of Pyrazinamide

Pyrazinamide is another first-line anti-mycobacterial drug that inhibits mycobacterial metabolism. Again, its mode of action remains to be elucidated fully. Pyrazinamide is used to treat tuberculosis. The drug is largely bacteriostatic, but can be bacteriocidal on actively replicating tuberculosis bacteria(McNeill L *et al.*2003).

Side Effect of Pyrazinamide: The most common (approximately 1%) side effect of pyrazinamide is joint pains (arthralgia), but this is not usually so severe that patients need to stop taking the pyrazinamide. Pyrazinamide can precipitate gout flares by decreasing renal excretion of uric acid (British Thoracic Society, 1984 and ATS doc,2003). The most dangerous side effect of pyrazinamide is hepatotoxicity, which is dose related. The old dose for pyrazinamide was 40–70 mg/kg daily and the incidence of drug-induced hepatitis has fallen significantly since the recommended dose has been reduced. In the standard four-drug regimen (isoniazid, rifampicin, pyrazinamide, ethambutol), pyrazinamide is the most common cause of drug-induced hepatitis.

Other side effects include nausea and vomiting, anorexia, sideroblastic anemia, skin rash, urticaria, pruritus, dysuria, interstitial nephritis, malaise; rarely porphyria, and fever (ATS doc,2003).

It's very unfortunate that after 1960s no drugs is discovered for tuberculosis treatment which have lesser side effects, less duration of treatment, more effectiveness against the *Mycobacterium tuberculosis* and its Multi-Drug resistant (MDR) strain.

The development of MDR strain and XDR (Extensively drug-resistant tuberculosis (XDR-TB) occur due to failure in treatment. After its development the first line drugs were not so effective and the chances of cure of the patient become lesser as compared to non MDR and non XDR tuberculosis patients on treatment (Extensively_drug-resistant_tuberculosis [online]accessed on 01-06-2014)

The side effects of treatment of tuberculosis make the treatment more and more troublesome for the patient and sometimes patient stops taking medicines before completion of treatment and results into development of MDR-TB. The American thoracic Society Documents official statement suggests that the anti tubercle drugs causes hepatotoxicity (ATS doc, March 2006). The Isoniazid causes Nausea, abdominal pain, Rifampicin causes hepatitis and flu like syndrome, Pyrazinamide causes GI symptoms, Arthralgias (joint pain), Rash, Hyperuricemia (elevated uric acid). To overcome these problems associated with these medications there is strong need from society to look over new possibilities for anti tubercle drugs and for this work herbs may be a good option to be exploited more for anti tubercle actions (Yee D *et al.*2003).

Role of herbal medicines in tuberculosis treatment

The traditional practice of herbal drugs comprise of medicinal plants, minerals, and organic matter; etc. Herbal drugs constitute only those traditional medicines, which primarily use plant preparations for therapy. The earliest recorded evidence of their use in Indians, Chinese, Egyptians, Greek, Roman and Syrian texts dates back to about 5000 years. The herbal/traditional medicine had been devised from rich traditions of ancient civilization and scientific heritage. Plant based active principles can be derived from any part of the plant like bark, leaves, flowers, roots, fruits, seeds, and the others.

Herbal medicine/material contains more active analogues or active principles also called as natural products such as alkaloids, flavonoids, terpenoids, essential oils, flower absolutes. Herbal medicines have a strong traditional or conceptual base and the potential to be useful as drugs in terms of safety and effectiveness leads for treating different diseases. World Health Organization (WHO) has made an attempt to identify all medicinal plants used globally and listed more than 20,000 species. According to the WHO more than 80% of the world's population realize on traditional herbal medicine for their primary health care.

Although herbal medicine has existed since the dawn of time, our knowledge of how plants actually affect human physiology remains largely unexplored. Numbers of plants are claiming various medicinal uses and a lot of research is going on in this view.

India is one among the 25 hotspots of the richest and highly endangered eco-regions of the world. Plants have been the major source of drugs in Indian system of medicine and other ancient systems in the world. The Indian tradition has an ancient heritage of traditional medicine. Indian traditional medicines based on various systems including Ayurveda, Siddha, Unani and Homeopathy. With the emerging worldwide interest in adopting and studying traditional systems and exploiting their potential based on different health care systems, the evaluation of the rich heritage of traditional medicine is essential.(Saha R, *et al.*2011)

Development of traditional herbal medicines into a modern drug of great therapeutic value is exemplified by the discovery of reserpine, a hypotensive drug from the roots of *rauwolfia serpentina* (Trease and Evans 1989). In year 2001, Iqbal *et.al* worked on Antimicrobial and phyto-chemical studies on 45 Indian medicinal plants against multi-drug resistant human pathogens.

There are list of plants which were traditional in therapeutic uses and medically important.

Table No. 03:- Ethno-botanical information of some traditionally used Indian medicinal plant species selected for antibacterial activity.

(Jigna Parekh, and Sumitra Chanda,2006)

Plant species	Family	Common name	Part used	Therapeutic use
Abutilon indicum L.	Malvaceae	Kansaki	Leaves	Rheumatism
Acorus calamus L.	Araceae	Vaj	Rhizomes	Flatulence, nervous disorders, diarrhoea
Ammannia baccifera L.	Lythraceae	Jal agio	Whole plant	Skin disorders

Argyrea nervosa Burm. F.	Convolvulaceae	Samudrasosh	Leaves	Ulcers, anorexia, bronchitis, inflammation
Bauhinia variegate L.	Caesalpiniaceae	Kanchnar	Bark	skin Diabetes, goiter, dysentery, diarrhoea
Crataeva religiosa Forst.	Cappparidaceae	Varun	Chaal Bark	skin Calculi, Flatulence, anaemia, heart complaints
Hedychium spicatum L.	Scitamineae	Kapur Kachli	Root	Nausea, bronchial asthama, local inflammation
Holarrhena antidysenterica L.	Apocynaceae	Kada	Chal Bark	skin dysentery, diarrhoea
Piper nigrum L.	Piperaceae	Chaval	Root	Stimulant, digestive, antispasmodic
Plumbego zeylanica L.	Plumbagenaceae	Chitrak	Root	Syphilis, leprosy, piles, rheumatism, leukoderma
Psoralea corylifolia L.	Leguminosae	Bavchi	Seeds	Leukoderma, leprosy, psoriasis
Saussurea lappa Costus.	Composite	Kuth or uplet	Root	Bronchitis, asthama, leprosy, flatulence

Table No.04 :- Showing List of plants tested for anti tuberculosis action on Lowenstein Jensen Medium

(Ref:-Renu Gupta *et al.* 2010)

Botanical Name/Family	Common Name	Part used	Extract
Acalypha indica L. *(Euphorbiacea)*	Acalypha	Leaf	Water Extract
Adhatoda vasica Nees. *(Acanthaseae)*	Vasaka	Leaf	Water Extract
Allium cepa L. *(Alliaceae)*	Onion	Bulb	Water Extract
Allium sativum L. *(Alliaceae)*	Garlic	Clove	Water Extract
Aloe vera L. *(Aloaceae)*	Aloevera	Leaf	Pure gel

CHAPTER FOUR

Plants useful in Tuberculosis

Abutilon indicum:

Taxonomic classification

Kingdom :- Plantae-Plants

Subkingdom :- Tracheobionta – Vascular plants

Super division :- Spermatophyta- seed plants

Division :- Magnoliophyta– Flowering plants

Class :- Magnoliopsida – Dicotyledons

Sub class :- Dilleniidae

Order :- Malvales

Family :- Malvaceae– Mallow family

Genus :- *Abutilon* Mill. – Indian mallow

Species :- *Abutilon indicum* (L.) Sweet – monkeybush

Description

Abutilon indicum is a member of the Malvaceae family. It is a shrub that can grow up to 2m high. The leaves are stalked measuring 2.5-10cm long with 2-7.5cm wide, ovate or orbiculate to cordate, irregularly crenate or dentate, acuminated, minutely hoary tomentose on both surfaces. The flowers are orange-yellow in colour, solitary, axillary. The fruiting carpels 15-20 in number, flat-topped, forming a head, measuring 2-2.5cm across, black and hairy. The fruits are hispid, scarcely longer than the calyx and the awns are erect. The seeds are three to five in number, kidney-shaped, dark brown or black in colour and with minutely stellate hairs. (http://www.globinmed.com [online] accessed on 19-05-2014)

Distribution

The species occurs in a number of tropical and subtropical zones. An example occurrence is within parts of the Great Barrier Reef islands of the Coral Sea (http://en.wikipedia.org[online]accessed on 19-05-2015)

Traditional medicinal usage

Tonic

Ancient Indian doctors including Charak and Sushruta made use of extract of the entire plant to promote vitality to their patients. They considered it a revitalizing nerving tonic and an aphrodisiac. The root was considered the better part for this purpose. In southern India the root is used for neurological disorders including treatment of hemiplagia, Bell's palsy, sciatica and debility. (C.P. Khare, 2004)

Gastrointestinal Diseases

The demulcent property of extracts of *A. indicum* is made use in the treatment of various gastrointestinal disorders. The extract together with clarified butter treats diarrhoea and biliousness (C.P. Khare, 2004) (K.M.Nadkarni, 1976).

The high fiber content of the leaves and the mucilaginous property is taken advantage in the treatment of haemorrhoids. A decoction of the leaves is a good mouth wash for toothaches and gum ailments. Finely powdered seeds are given as a laxative.

Respiratory Diseases

The powdered flowers of *A. indicum* are a remedy for cough as recommended by the Ayurvedic and Unani systems. In the west it is the roots that is used to protect the respiratory system. A decoction of it is given to treat bronchitis and chest pains.

Genito-urinary Diseases

Western herbal medicine believed *A. indicum* has protective properties towards the urinary system. The roots are considered diuretic and its decoction is given for all types of dysurias. It is the medicine prescribed by Unani practitioners for strangury, polyuria and haematuria. The seeds on the other hand were given to treat impotency and spermatorrhoea. The seeds are distinctly useful in gonorrhoea, gleet and chronic cystitis. The leaves and roots too could be used to treat gonorrhoea and other forms of urethritis.

Other uses

The powdered herb was used for meno-metrorrhagia. The leaves are used to treat various skin diseases including wounds and ulcers while the seeds are used for leprosy. In Nepals the infusion of the roots is employed for leprosy. In China the plant is used to treat deafness, tinnitus and earache, colds, high fever, mumps, hives, pulmonary tuberculosis, anuria, carbuncle, hernia. (*Abutilon indicum* [online] accessed on 19-05-2014)

Pharmacological study:-

Antidiabetic activity

Seetharam *et al.*(2002) found that both the aqueous and alcoholic extracts of the leaves of *A. indicum* had significant hypoglycaemic effects in normal rats 4 hours after administration. Adisakwattan *et al.*(2009) further looked into the alcoholic (methanol) leaf extract's hypoglycaemic activity and observed that the extract was able to suppress the postprandial hyperglycaemia by inhibiting a-glucosidase and sucrase activities in the intestine. The effects of aqueous leaf extract showed that in addition to inhibition of α-glucosidase and sucrase, this extract was found to stimulate the insulin production by the b-cells of the pancreas (Krisanapun C, *et al.* 2009) .

Hepatoprotective activity :-

The aqueous extract of *A. indicum* showed significant hepatoprotective activity when it was found the it was able to reduce biochemical parameter changes as a result of exposure of experimental rats to CCl_4 and Paracetamol (Porchezhian E,2005) .

Analgesic activity

Eugenol was isolated from *A. indicum* using bioactivity guided isolation. Eugenol was found to possess the ability to inhibit acetic acid induced writhing in mice and prolonged tail flicking time (Ahmed M, *et al.*2000) this indicates that the extract posses significant analgesic activity via both peripheral and central mechanism.

Immunomodulatory activity

Aqueous and ethanol extracts of the leaves of *A. indicum* were assessed for the immunomodulatory activity using various animal models. The results showed that there was significant increase in the production of circulating antibody titre in response to sheep red blood cells, increase in both primary and secondary haemagglutination antibody, a significant potentiation of delayed type hypersensitivity reaction. There was also a significant increase in percentage of neutrophils adhesion to nylon fibre and phagocytic activity. The results indicate that the extracts were able to trigger both specific and non-specific immunological activity and that this could be attributed to the flavonoids content (Dashputre N. L. *et al.* 2010).

Antimicrobial activity

Methanolic extract of the leaves of *A. indicum* was found to have remarkable antifungal activity against *Trichophyton rubrum*. This activity may be due to the presence of flavonoids in the extract especially Quercetin (Rajalakshmi Padma Vairavasundaram, 2009).

Antioxidant activity

Yasmin *et al.* (2010) studied the antioxidant activity of organic solvent extracts of aerial parts and roots of *A. indicum*. They found that all the extracts contain both slow reacting and fast reacting antioxidant.

Chemical constituents of the plant

Gallic acid, asparagine, fructose, galactose, glucose, beta-sitosterone, vanillic acid, p-coumaric acid, p-hydroxybenzoic acid, caffeic acid, fumaric acid, p-beta-D-glycosyloxybenzoic acid, leucine, histidine, threonine, serine, glutamic acid, aspartic acid and galacturonic acid, alantolactone, isoalantolactone, threonine, glutamine, serine, proline, glycine, alanine, cycteine, methionine, isoleucine, valine, leucine, tyrosine, phenylalanine, histidine, lysine, arginine.

Allium cepa:

Taxonomic classification

Kingdom :- Plantae-Plants
Subkingdom :- Tracheobionta – Vascular plants
Super division :- Spermatophyta- seed plants
Division :- Magnoliophyta– Flowering plants
Class :- Liliopsida – Monocotyledons
Sub class :- Liliidae
Order :- Liliales
Family :- Liliaceae– Lily family
Genus :- *Allium* L.
Species :- *Allium cepa*

(https://plants.usda.gov/java/ClassificationServlet?source=profile&symbol=ALLIU&display=63[online]accessed on 20-052014)

Description

The onion (*Allium cepa*) (Latin 'cepa' = onion), also known as the bulb onion or common onion, is used as a vegetable and is the most widely cultivated species of the genus *Allium*. This genus also contains several other species variously referred to as onions and cultivated for food. It was first officially described by Carolus Linnaeus in his 1753 work Species Plantarum (Brewster, James L.1994). The onion plant (*Allium cepa*) is unknown in the wild but has been grown and selectively bred in cultivation for at least 7,000 years. It is a biennial plant but is usually grown as annual. Modern varieties typically grow to a height of 15 to 45 cm (6 to 18 in). The leaves are blueish-green and grow alternately in a flattened, fan-shaped swathe. They are fleshy, hollow and cylindrical, with one flattened side. They are at their broadest about a quarter of the way up beyond which they taper towards a blunt tip. The base of each leaf is a flattened, usually white sheath that grows out of a basal disc. From the underside of the disc, a bundle of fibrous roots extends for a short way into the soil. As the onion matures, food reserves begin to accumulate in the leaf bases and the bulb of the onion swells.

In the autumn the leaves die back and the outer scales of the bulb become dry and brittle, and this is the time at which the crop is normally harvested. If left in the soil over winter, the growing point in the middle of the bulb begins to develop in the spring. New leaves appear and a long, stout, hollow stem expands, topped by a bract protecting a developing inflorescence. The inflorescence takes the form of a globular umbel of white flowers with parts in sixes. The seeds are glossy black and triangular in cross section. (Brickell, Christopher,1992)

Distribution

Common onions are normally available in three colour varieties. *Yellow* or *brown* onions (called *red* in some European countries), are full-flavoured and are the onions of choice for everyday use. Yellow onions turn a rich, dark brown when caramelized and give French onion soup its sweet flavour. The *red* onion (called *purple* in some European countries) is a good choice for fresh use when its colour livens up the dish. It is also used in grilling and char-broiling. *White* onions are the traditional onions that are used in classic Mexican cuisine. While the large mature onion bulb is the onion most often eaten, onions can be eaten at immature stages. Young plants may be harvested before bulbing occurs and used whole as scallions. When an onion is harvested after bulbing has begun but the onion is not yet mature, the plants are sometimes referred to as *summer* onions.

Additionally, onions may be bred and grown to mature at smaller sizes. Depending on the mature size and the purpose for which the onion is used, these may be referred to as *pearl*, *boiler*, or *pickler* onions, but differ from true pearl onions which are a different species. Pearl and boiler onions may be cooked as a vegetable rather than as an ingredient and pickler onions are often preserved in vinegar as a long-lasting relish.

Onions are available in fresh, frozen, canned, caramelized, pickled and chopped forms. The dehydrated product is available as kibbled, sliced, rings, minced, chopped, granulated and powder forms. Onion powder is a spice widely used when the fresh ingredient is not available. It is made from finely ground, dehydrated onions, mainly the pungent varieties of bulb onions, and has a strong odour. Being dehydrated, it has a long shelf life and comes in several varieties: yellow, red and white.

Traditional medicinal usage

Due to the anti-inflammatory agents in onions they help reduce the severity of symptoms associated with conditions such as the pain and swelling of the osteo- and rheumatoid arthritis, the allergic inflammatory response of asthma, and the respiratory congestion associated with common colds. The onions anti-inflammatory effects are not only due to their vitamin C and quercetin, but other active components called isothiocyanates have made onions a good ingredient for soups and stews during cold and flu season. WHO recommends the use of fresh onion extracts for treating coughs, colds, asthma, bronchitis and also relieving hoarseness. The World Health Organization also supports the use of onions for the treatment of appetite loss and preventing atherosclerosis.

Pharmacological study

The fleshy bulb that grows below the ground is used medicinally as well as for food. Onion is believed to have a positive effect on the circulatory system. It has been used as a diuretic to reduce swelling. It is also thought to help reduce arteriosclerosis by lowering blood cholesterol levels and preventing the formation of blood clots. Onion has been used to treat diabetes and is reputed to lower blood sugar levels. Externally; fresh onion juice is used to prevent bacterial and fungal infections. It can be applied to wounds and stings on the skin, used to remove warts, used to stimulate hair growth, and even used to reduce unwanted skin blemishes. Warm onion juice dropped in the ear is said to help relieve earache. Baked onion is used to draw pus from abscesses. The onion also may be of benefit in cardiovascular disease, as it possesses hypo-lipidemic effects and has anti-platelet actions, retarding thrombosis. But certain lipid-reducing and blood pressure-lowering effects in humans have not yet been clinically proven. Some studies have been performed concerning diabetes treatment by onion with promising results in animal experimentation. Although more research is needed on the use of onion as a treatment for diabetes in humans, many articles describe onion's benefits in improving glucose levels. The onion also is a proven antioxidant and may be helpful in treating certain cancers.

Green Onion as Alternative Medicine

- It is mainly used as a traditional medicine for common cold.
- It stimulates the respiratory tract and helps in expelling sputum (phlegm).
- It contains essential oils that stimulates the sweat glands and promote sweating.
- It normalizes blood pressure.
- It increases appetite.
- It helps prevent diarrhea.
- It is rich in sulfur, an essential element that kills or inhibits fungus infections.
- It inhibits cancer cell growth especially colon cancer. Green onion's anti- colon cancer properties are well known among traditional healers around the world.
- It contains vitamin A and C. The white part of it has calcium, too.
- It is a good appetizer. (K. P. Sampath Kumar *et al.* 2010)

Health benefits of Onion include substantial relief from number of diseases such as common cold, asthma, bacterial infections, respiratory problems, angina, and cough. Onions are also known to repel blood thirsty insects. In other words, you may say that onions are godsend gifts. Onions are known to possess curative value from ancient time.

Hepatoprotective activity

It was reported that *A. cepa* leaf extract also can significantly restored the elevated AST, ALT and ALP enzyme levels to the normal levels(S.F. Ige, *et al.* 2011).Recently, Riyaz Shaik *et al.* (2012) demonstrated that *A. cepa* leaves protected hepatocytes by preventing the release of these 3 enzymes. The study of B.Ogunlade *et al.*(2012) demonstrated that administration of *A. cepa* by rabbits with alcohol abuse remarkably reduced serum levels of liver biomarker enzymes. In the study, performed by K. Eswar Kumar *et al.* 2013, demonstrated that *A. cepa* aqueous bulb extract had reduced levels of AST, ALT and ALP which were elevated by ethanol administration.

Antimicrobial activity

In 2009 Chitra Shenoy *et al.* described about the preliminary phytochemical investigation and wound healing activity of *Allium cepa* Linn (Lilaceae) Renu Gupta *et al.* 2010 described that exhibited activity against MDR isolates of *M. tuberculosis* in her research entitled Anti-tuberculosis activity of selected medicinal plants against multi-drug resistant *Mycobacterium tuberculosis* isolates. Jain RC, 1993 and Ratnakar P, Murthy PS,1996 in their study confirms that the *Allium cepa* has the anti-tubercle activity. *Allium cepa* have the anti tubercle activity as studied by Sivakumar A and Jayaraman G in 2011.

In the year 1999 a monograph was published by WHO on selected medicinal plants VOLUME 1 in which *A. cepa* is considered to have antibacterial property against tuberculosis. N. Benkeblia (2004) discussed on Antimicrobial activity of essential oil extracts of various onions (*Allium cepa*) and garlic (*Allium sativum*). Ivan A. Ross (2005) in his book Medicinal Plants *of the* World Volume 3 *Chemical Constituents, Traditional and Modern Medicinal Uses* describe the medicinal property of *A. cepa* for tuberculosis.

Vikrant Arya (2011) in his "A Review on Anti-Tubercular Plants" describe the antibacterial property for tuberculosis, later on in 2013 Soundhari C and Rajarajan S worked *in vitro* screening of lyophilized extracts of alpinia galangal L. and *Oldenlandia umbellata L.* for anti-mycobacterial activity and described Water and ethanolic extracts of selected medicinal plants (*A. sativum* -bulb, *A. cepa* -tissue, *S. aromaticum* –flowerbud, *C. verum* -bark) observed to have anti-TB activity for *M. tuberculosis* H37Ra by Microtiter Alamar Blue assay and confirmed to (Sivakumar A and Jayaraman G 2011). M. Muthuswamy (2013) described that *Allium cepa* and *Aloe vera* were selected to test their activity further against MDR trains of *M. tuberculosis*, while selection of *Acalypha indica* was based on its ethno-medicinal uses in respiratory disorder. *A. cepa* was selected on the basis of knowledge that *A. sativum* has anti-tuberculosis activity; therefore other species of *Allium* might also have anti- tuberculosis activity in his study of screening of anti-tubercular activity of some medicinal plants from Western Ghats of India.

Water and ethanolic extracts of selected medicinal plants (*A. sativum* -bulb, *A. cepa* -tissue, *S. aromaticum* –flowerbud, *C. verum* -bark) observed to have anti-TB activity for *M. tuberculosis* H37Ra by Microtiter Alamar Blue assay (Sivakumar A and Jayaraman G 2011). Onion has the property of anti-cancer and anti-oxidant because of presence of phenols and flavonoids. It is rich in proteins, carbohydrates, sodium, potassium and phosphorous. It has been reported to be an anti-bacterial, antiviral, anti-parasitic, anti-fungal and has hypoglycemic, antithrombotic, anti-hyperlipidemic, anti-inflammatory and antioxidant activity (Parmar Namita and Rawat Mukesh,2012).

Antioxidant activity

Phenolic compounds are the major group contributing to the antioxidant activity of vegetables, fruit, cereals and other plant-based materials. The antioxidant activity of the compounds is partly due to one electron reduction potential that is the ability to act as hydrogen or electron donors.(Chan *et al.*2007)

The findings of the study by Siti Fairuz Che Othman *et al.*(2011) have shown that red onion (*A. cepa L.*) possesses higher Total phenolic content (TPC) than garlic (*A. sativum L.*).

Chemical constituents of the plant

Onions not only provide flavor, they also provide important nutrients and health-promoting phytochemicals. High in vitamin C, onions are a good source of dietary fiber, and folic acid. They also contain calcium, iron, and have a high protein quality (ratio of mg amino acid/gram protein). Onions are low in sodium and contain no fat. Onions contain quercetin, a flavonoid (one category of antioxidant compounds). Antioxidants are compounds that help delay or slow the oxidative damage to cells and tissue of the body. Studies have indicated that quercetin helps to eliminate free radicals in the body, to inhibit low-density lipoprotein oxidation (an important reaction in the atherosclerosis and coronary heart disease), to protect and regenerate vitamin E (a powerful antioxidant), and to inactivate the harmful effects of chelate metal ions. (http://onions-usa.org/all-about-onions/onion-health-research[online] accessed on 20-05-2014)

***Pheonix dectylefera* (Date palm)**

Taxonomic classification

Kingdom :- Plantae-Plants
Subkingdom :- Tracheobionta – Vascular plants
Super division :- Spermatophyta- seed plants
Division :- Magnoliophyta– Flowering plants
Class :- Liliopsida – Monocotyledons
Sub class :- Arecidae
Order :- Arecales
Family :- Arecaceae – Palm family
Genus :- *Phoenix* L. – date palm
Species :- *Phoenix dactylifera* L. – date palm

(https://plants.usda.gov/core/profile?symbol=PHDA4#[online] accessed on 20-05-2014)

Description

Phoenix dectylefera (Date palm) belongs to Arecaceae family and grown in the middle East since at least 6000 BC (Copley M.S. *et al.*2001). The palm with a very slender trunk, up to 30 m tall, conspicuously covered with the remains of sheaths from fallen leaves. Its leaves, clustered together in a maximum number of 20-30 and forming a loose crownshaft, are pinnate, up to 6 m long, upper leaves are ascending, basal leaves are recurved, the segments are coriaceous, linear, rigid and sharp pointed, blue-green in colour.

Its flowers, unisexual on dioecious plants, are small, whitish, fragrant, clustered in axillary spadices up to 120 cm long markedly bent downwards by their fruit weight. These fruits, commonly known as dates, are oblong berries, dark-orange when ripe, up to 50 cm long in the cultivated varieties, their flesh is sacchariferous, and it contains one woody seed.

Distribution

The date palm, native to North Africa has been extensively cultivated here as well as in Arabia and as far as the Persian Gulf, where it features as the characteristic vegetation of oases. Moreover it is grown over the Canary Islands, in the northern Mediterranean and in the south of the United States.

Traditional medicinal usage

The different parts of this plant is majorly used in conventional medicine for treatment of various disorders like memory instability, fever, pain, stammering , nervous disorders(Nadkarni K.M.1976). Fatmah H (2013) discussed on Effect of Tempeh Dates Biscuits on Nutritional Status of Preschool Children with Tuberculosis.

Date Fruits To Provide Relieve From:

- Sore throat
- Colds
- Throat and chest infections by mixing equal amount of dates, fig, hibiscus and raisin and boiled in water. Use as expectorant.
- Fever
- Bronchial asthma by mixing dates with fenugreek
- Use as astringent for intestinal problem
- Counteracting alcohol intoxication
- Use as aphrodisiac by mixing dates with milk and cinnamon
- Poisonous effect by applying date paste onto the poisonous bite area

(http://hubpages.com/hub/The-Various-Uses-of-Date-Palm-Tree[online] accessed on 20-05-2014)

Pharmacological study:-

Antifungal activity

Antifungal activity of water, acetone and methanol extracts of leaves and pits of *phoenix dectylifera* Linn. were evaluated against several pathogenic fungi by Bokhari NA *et al.* in 2012. Except water extract acetone and methanol extracts showed varying degree of growth inhibitors against *Fusarium oxysporum,Fusarium species and Fusarium solani.*

Anti-hyperlipedemic Activity

Coronary heart disease is related to decrease in the concentrations of high density lipoprotein cholesterol(HDL) and increase of low density lipoprotein cholesterol(LDL). Salah and Al miaman (2013) have reported that feedeing of defatted date seed flour containing diet at 1.5%, 2.5%, and 5.2% to rats reduced the plasma triglycerides, total cholesterol and low density liporoteins.

Anti-ulcer activity

Pre-treatment with date fruit ethanolic and aqueous extracts at a dose of 4 ml/kg for 14 days markedly ameliorated the ulcer index, histological indices such as necrosis, haemorrhage, congestion and oedema in stomach sections and biochemical levels of some enzymes such as gastrin in plasma and mucin and histamine in gastric mucosa of ethanol-induced gastric ulceration in rats.(Al-Qarawi A, *et al.*2005)This support to the local folk medicinal claim that dates may be useful to humans with ulcers.

Anticancer activity

The polysaccharides (glucans) prepared from the date fruits exhibited a dose dependant anticancer activity with an optimum activity at a dose of 1 mg/kg in tumour induced by subcutaneously transplanting allogenic solid Sarcoma-180 tumor cells into the right side of female CD1 mice. (Ishurda O, *et al.* 2005) This research validated the traditional claim of date fruits to be used against various kinds of tumors.

Anti-diarrhoeal Activity:

Aqueous extract of *Phoenix dactylifera L* at doses of 3, 6 and 12 mg/kg produced a statistically significant reduction in both castor oil induced intestinal transit and frequency of diarrhoea in rat(Abdulla Y, Al –Taher,2008). These properties may explain the rational for the effective use of the plant as an anti-diarrhoeal agent in traditional medicine.

Effect on gastrointestinal transit

Water and ethanolic extracts from date flesh and date pits at doses of 0.01, 0.02 and 0.04 ml/kg showed a dose dependant increase in the gastrointestinal transit time. While water extract from dialyzed date flesh extract induced a dose-dependent decrease the gastrointestinal transit time. (Al-Qarawi AA, *et al.*2003) The possible reason for this may be the method based extraction of pirticular component which could be valuable towards respective clinical conditions.

Effect on reproductive system

Oral administration of date palm fruit suspensions at doses of 120 and 240 mg/kg improved the sperm count, motility, morphology, and DNA quality with a concomitant increase in the weights of testis and epididymis. (Bahmanpour S, *et al.* 2006) Moreover, date extracts have been shown to increase sperm count in guinea pigs and to enhance spermatogenesis and increase the concentration of testosterone, follicle stimulating hormone (FSH) and luteininzing hormone (LH) in rats. (Elgasim EA *et al.* 1995) This study suggests its usefulness in solving infertility problems in males. El-Desoky and his co-workers (1995) looked into the effect of date palm pollen grains (*Phoenix dactylifera*) on sexual hormonal balance, cholesterol, total lipids, total protein, albumin, globulin, and liver functions in control male and female rats, and castrated and ovariectomized rats. Their findings showed a decline in serum testostrerone level; in control male rats, but a slight increase was detected in the castrated rats. Similarly, serum estradiol content was elevated in both control and ovariectomised rats. Progesterone level; however, decreased in control female rats, and was slightly increased in ovariectomized rats, with slight increase of serum FSH and LH in both normal and ovariectomised female rats. Pollen grains significantly increased serum globulin, total protein and total lipids in ovariectomized rats. Also serum ALP activity was increased in normal male rats. There was an increase in serum plasma glutamate pyruvate (GPT) activity in normal male, ovariectomized female and castrated rats, and similarly, glutamate oxaloacetate transaminase (GOT) activity was also increased in overiectomized female and normal male rats. All these GPT and GOT values were still within the normal range in rats (Reshod A, Al-

Shagrawi, 1998).

Nephroprotective activity

Al-Qarawi (2008) *et al.* studied the effect of the extracts of the flesh and pits of Phoenix dactylifera on gentamicin induced nephrotoxicity in rats was investigated in which the significantly reduced the increase in plasma creatinine and urea concentrations induced by gentamycin nephrotoxicity and ameliorated the proximal tubular damage. Antioxidant components in the date (e.g., melatonin, vitamin E, and ascorbic acid) were suggested to be the basis of the nephroprotection.

(http://ispub.com/IJPHARM/7/1/8733[online]accessed on 24-05-2014)

Hepatoprotective activity:

Pre and post treatment with aqueous extract of date flesh or pits significantly reduced CCl4 induced elevation in plasma activities of aspartate aminotransferase (AST), alanine aminotransferase (ALT), Alkaline phosphatase (ALP) enzymes and bilirubin concentration and ameliorated morphological and histological liver damage in rats. This study suggests that CCl4-induced liver damage in rats can be reversed by treatment of extracts from date flesh or pits. Moreover it can also be used prophylactically as a dynamic liver support GT (Al-Qarawi AA, *et al.*2004), enzymes and plasma concentration of bilirubin but also exhibited an enormous increase in the reduced serum levels of testosterone, alpha fetoprotein (AFP) and glucose in the thioacetamide induced chirrotic rats. The extracts also showed significant reduction in oxidative stress evidenced by significant rise in the hepatic malonaldehyde (MDA) levels and decline in hepatic glutathione levels by normalising them. In another study the date flesh or pit extracts not only normalised the elevated plasma activities of AST, ALT, ALP, lactate dehydrogenase (LDH).

H.A. Abdelrahman *et al.* in 2012 also studied the protective effect of dates(*Phoenix dectylifera*) on carbon tetrachloride induced hepatotoxicity in Dogs.

Antioxidant activity:

Phytochemicals from fruits have been shown to possess significant antioxidant capacities that may be associated with lower incidence and lower mortality rates of degenerative diseases in human(Javanmardi J, *et al.*2008).

Various *in vitro* and *in vivo* antioxidant activites have been carried out on various extracts of different parts of *Phoenix dectylefera.* Studies conducted on antioxidant activity and phenolic content of various fruits of *Phoenix dactylifera* cultivated in Iran, Algeria and Bahrain demonstrated a linear relationship between antioxidant activity and the total phenolic content (TPC) of date fruit extract(Allaith, Abdul AA,2005). Aqueous date extract was found to inhibit significantly the lipid peroxidation and protein oxidation and also exhibited a potent superoxide and hydroxyl radical scavenging activity in a dose-dependent manner in an in vitro study(Dammak I *et al.* 2007). Methanolic extract of Phoenix dectylefera seeds showed a significant increase in plasma levels of vitamin C, E and A, β-carotene and significant decrease in the elevated MDA levels due to the lipid peroxidation in adjuvant arthritis in rats. (Mohamed DA *et al.*2004) These findings suggests its possible use in diseases such as scurvy, ataxia and night blindness caused due to the deficiency of vitamins C, E and A respectively. Date seed oil was found to limit oxidative injuries induced by hydrogen peroxide in human skin organ culture which confirmed the potent free radical scavenging activity of the plant(Dammak I *et al.* 2007).

Studies indicate that the aqueous extracts of dates have potent antioxidant activity (Mansouri *et al.*2005). The antioxidant activity is attributed to the wide range of phenolic compounds in dates including p-coumaric, ferulic and sinapic acids, flavonoids and procyanidins (Gu *et al.*2003 and Al-Farsi *et al.*2005).

Antimicrobial activity

The anti bacterial study on *Pheonix dectylefera* carried out by Ramesa Shafi Bhat *et al.* andSaleh FA, *et al.* observed the extracts of fruit showed the antibacterial activity against the human pathogen such as *S.aureus, S. pyogenes, B.subtillis ,E. coli* and *P. aeruginosa* and *Staphylococcus saprophyticus* (Ramesa Shafi Bhat *et al.*2012, Saleh FA).

Chemical constituents of the plant

The fruits of *Phoenix dactylifera* contain different chemical compounds such as saturated and unsaturated fatty acids, Zinc (Zn), Cadmium (Cd), Calcium (Ca), and potassium (K). Saturated fatty acids include stearic and palmitic acid and unsaturated fatty Acids contain linoleic and oleic acids which could inhibit 5 -α reeducates enzyme (Shariati *et al.* 2008). Also, dates contain at least six vitamins including a small amount of vitamin C, and vitamins B1 (thiamine), B2 (riboflavin), nicotinic acid (niacin) and vitamin A (Al-Shahib and Marshall,1993).

Dates contain a high percentage of carbohydrate (total sugars, 44-88%), protein (2.3-5.6%), fat (0.2-9.3%), essential salts and minerals, vitamins and an elevated proportion of dietary fiber (6.4-11.5%) (El Hadrami *et al.* 2009). They also contain oil in the flesh (0.2-0.5%) and the seed (7.7-9.7%). The seed represents 5.6-14.2% of the entire fruit weight. Dates are very rich in vitamins, especially β-carotene (vitamin A), thiamine (B1), riboflavin (B2), niacin, ascorbic acid (C) and folic acid (folacin) (El Hadrami, 2009). Some of these vitamins provide 10-50% of the daily recommended intake of an adult. Ripe fruits were reported to contain a substantial amount of carotenoids including lutein and various forms of β-carotene and minor carotenoids. The contents vary with the cultivar and stage of ripeness, with the total content of carotenoids decreasing towards the final ripening stages and in storage.

Andrographis peniculata :

Description

A. paniculata, also known as Chirayetah or Chiretta and Kalmegh. It is an annual plant, 1-3 ft high, that is one of the most commonly used plants in the traditional systems of Unani and Ayurvedic medicines. It is called Creat in English and is known as the "king of bitters." (Kabeeruddin M.1937, Dymock W.1972).

Taxonomic classification:-

Kingdom :- Plantae-Plants
Subkingdom :- Viridaeplantae – green plants
Super division :- Spermatophyta- seed plants
Division :- Tracheophyta – vascular plants, tracheophytes
Class :- Magnoliopsida
Order :- Lamiales
Family :- Acanthaceae
Genus :- Andrographis Wall. ex Nees – false waterwillow
Species :- Andrographis paniculata (Burm. f.) Wall. ex Nees

(http://www.itis.gov/servlet/SingleRpt/SingleRpt?search_topic=TSN&search_value=184881 [online] accessed on 24-05-2014)

Distribution

A. paniculata is distributed in tropical Asian countries, often in isolated patches. It can be found in a variety of habitats, such as plains, hillsides, coastlines, and disturbed and cultivated areas such as roadsides, farms, and wastelands. Native populations of *A. paniculata* are spread throughout south India and Sri Lanka which perhaps represent the center of origin and diversity of the species. The herb is an introduced species in northern parts of India, Java, Malaysia, Indonesia, the West Indies, and elsewhere in the Americas. The species also occurs in Hong Kong, Thailand, Brunei, Singapore, and other parts of Asia where it may or may not be native. The plant is cultivated in many areas, as well.

Unlike other species of the genus, *A. paniculata* is of common occurrence in most places in India, including the plains and hilly areas up to 500 m, which accounts for its wide use.

Traditional medicinal usage

Andrographis paniculata is a plant that has been effectively used in traditional Asian medicines for centuries. Its perceived "blood purifying" property results in its use in diseases where blood "abnormalities" are considered causes of disease, such as skin eruptions, boils, scabies, and chronic undetermined fevers. Controlled clinical trials report its safe and effective use for reducing symptoms of uncomplicated upper respiratory tract infections. Since many of the disease conditions commonly treated with *A. paniculata* in traditional medical systems are considered self-limiting, its purported benefits need critical evaluation.

(*A. paniculata* http://altmedrev.com/publications/16/1/66.pdf[online] accessed on 24-05-2014)

A. paniculata contains diterpenes, lactones, and flavonoids. Flavonoids mainly exist in the root, but have also been isolated from the leaves. "The aerial parts contain alkanes, ketones, and aldehydes. Although, it was initially thought that the bitter substance in the leaves was the lactone andrographolide, later investigations showed that the leaves contained two bitter principles – andrographolide and a compound named kalmeghin. Four lactones

– chuanxinlian A (deoxyandrographolide), B (andrographolide), C (neoandrographolide) and D (14-deoxy-11, 12-didehydroandrographolide) – were isolated from the aerial parts in China. *A. Peniculata* contains diterpene glucoside (deoxyandrographolide- 19beta-D-glucoside) has been detected in the leaves (Weiming C,1982) and six diterpenoids of the ent-labdane type, two diterpene glucosides and four diterpene dimers (bis-andrographolides A, B, C, and D) have been isolated from aerial parts(Matsuda T,1994).

A. paniculata is extensively used as a hepatostimulant and hepatoprotective agent in Indian systems of medicine (Trivedi NP, *et al.* 2001). *A. paniculata* is also an ingredient in several polyherbal preparations used as hepatoprotectants in India, (Ram VJ,2001) one of which has been reported as efficacious in chronic hepatitis B virus infection (Rajkumar JS,2007). S.K. Mitra *et al.* (1998) described Protective effect of HD-03, a herbal formulation, against various hepatotoxic agents in rats. Rakshamani Tripathi *et al.* (2005) worked on Modulation of oxidative damage by natural products. Shahid Akbar, MD, PhD (2011) reviewed the *Andrographis paniculata* in his monograph about the Pharmacological Activities and Clinical Effects. G. Shivaprakash (2011) described the Evaluation of *Andrographis paniculata* leaves extract for analgesic activity. Anil Kumar (2012) worked on *Andrographis paniculata* and review on king of bitter (Kalmegh with the result *Andrographis paniculata* nees (Acanthaceae) is a medicinal plant traditionally used for the treatment of anti-inflammatory, antibacterial, antioxidant, antiparasitic, antispasmodic, antidiabatic, anti-carcinogenic, antipyretic, antidiarrhoeal, hepatoprotective, nematocidal.

Pharmacological study

Andrographis paniculata has been reported as having antibacterial, antifungal, antiviral, choleretic, hypoglycemic, hypocholesterolemic, adaptogenic, anti-inflammatory, emollient, astringent, diuretic, carminative, anthelmintic, antipyretic, gastric and liver tonic. It is also recommended for use in cases of leprosy, gonorrhea, scabies, boils, skin eruptions, and chronic and seasonal fevers. Juice or an infusion of fresh leaves is given to infants to relieve griping, irregular bowel habits, and loss of appetite. Leaves and root are also used in general debility, during convalescence after fevers, for dyspepsia associated with gaseous distension, and in advanced stages of dysentery. In China, the herb derived from the leaves or aerial parts of Andrographis *paniculata* is known as Chuanxinlian, Yijianxi or Lanhelian. It is described as bitter and cold, is considered to be antipyretic, detoxicant, anti-inflammatory, and detumescent, and is thought to remove "pathogenic heat" from the blood. *Andrographis paniculata* is used for the treatment of pharyngolaryngitis, diarrhea, dysentery, and cough with thick sputum, carbuncle, sores, and snake bites. Various preparations and compound formulas of the herb have been used to treat infectious and non-infectious diseases, with significant effective rates reported for conditions such as epidemic encephalitis B, suppurative otitis media, neonatal subcutaneous annular ulcer, vaginitis, cervical erosion, pelvic inflammation, herpes zoster, chicken pox, mumps, neurodermatitis, eczema, and burns. A primary modern use of *Andrographis paniculata* is for the prevention and treatment of the common cold. It appears to have antithrombotic actions, suggesting a possible benefit in cardiovascular disease. Pharmacological and clinical studies suggest the potential for beneficial effects in diseases like cancer and HIV infections.

Hepatoprotective activity

Soumendra Darbar *et al.* (2009) described the antioxidant and hepatoprotective action of *Andrographis paniculata* by induction of hepatotoxicity in rats using single doe of Diclofan (DIC). The results of the study concluded that the hepatoprotective effect of aqueous ethanol extract of *Andrographis paniculata* against DIC –induced acute toxicity is mediated either by preventing the decline of hepatic antioxidant status or due to its direct radical scavenging capacity.

Antimicrobial activity

Andrographis paniculata has been extensively shows antimicrobial and antiparasitic activities such as bacteria, viruses, and parasites. Singha *et al.* (2007) reported significant antibacterial activity of an aqueous extract and attributed it to the combined effect of andrographolides and arabinogalactan proteins. A similar conclusion was reached by Zaidan *et al.* (2005) found crude aqueous extract of leaves exhibit significant antimicrobial activity against gram positive *S. aureus*, methicillin-resistant *S.aureus* and gram-negative *Pseudomonas aeruginosa*, but had no activity against *Escherichia coli* or *Klebsiella pneumoniae*. Andrographolide, neoandrographolide, and 14-deoxy-11, 12-didehydroandrographolide are reported to be viricidal against herpes simplex virus 1 (HSV-1) without having any significant cytotoxicity at viricidal concentrations. Alcoholic extract of the rhizome was reported to possess significant *in vitro* activity against *Ascaris lumbricoides* and chloroform extract completely inhibited malarial parasitic growth within 24 hours of incubation at a concentration of 0.05 mg/mL. Same inhibition was achieved in 48 hours with methanol extract at a concentration of 2.5 mg/mL. (Anil Kumar *et al.*2012)

Antioxidant activity

The main and most interesting biological constituent of *A. paniculata* herb (aerial part) is a group of diterpene lactones belonging to the ent-labdane class, present in both free and glycosidic forms, and named andrographolides(Lim, J. C, *et al.*2012). Andrographolide is the bitter principle, a colourless, neutral crystalline substance, was first isolated by Boorsma from different parts of *Andrographis paniculata*. In 1911 Gorter proved that it is structurally a lactone and named it andrographolide (in the Chinese literature it is sometimes cited as andrographis B). (María A *et al.* 2013).

The second diterpene isolated from *A. paniculata* was the minor non-bitter constituent neoandrographolide, which was first described by Kleipool in 1952. The structure of neoandrographolide was described as a diterpene glucoside and its amount in the plant is around 0.5-1%. The main preclinical effects are anti-inflammatory (Parichatikanond *et al.*2010, Batkhuu *et al.*2002, Liu, J *et al.*2007), chemosensitizer, anti-herpes-simplex virus and antioxidant.

Chemical constituents of the plant

The plant is widely used in ayurvedic and homeopathic systems of medicines. The medicinal value of this plant is due to the presence of active ingredients *viz* andrographolide and neoandrographolide which are derivatives of diterpenoids. It prevents oxidative damage and inhibits binding to toxic metabolites to DNA.

CHAPTER FIVE

Materials and Methods

All the chemicals used in the present investigation were of analytical grade and obtained from Sigma Chemical Co. St. Louis Mo. USA; SRL Pvt. Ltd., Mumbai; Himedia Laboratories Pvt. Ltd; and S. D. fine chemicals Pvt. Ltd., Mumbai.

1. Collection of plant materials

A. *Phoenix dactylifera* (Fruits): Fruits of this plant were collected during Jan 2005 from the local areas of Nagpur region, India.

B. *Andrographis peniculata* (Leaves): Leaves were collected during Feb. 2005 from the local areas in Nagpur region, India.

C. *Allium cepa* (Bulbs): Plant material bulbs were collected from the Local areas in Nagpur region, India during of Mar.2005.

D. *Abutilon indicum* (Leaves and Seeds): Leaves and seeds of this plant were collected during May 2005 from the local areas in Nagpur region, India.

2. Identification and authentication of plant Species

The authentic identification of the plant species were carried out at P.G. Department of Botany, Rashtrasant Tukadoji Maharaj Nagpur University, Nagpur, (M.S.) India as per the reference numbers allotted by the department.

Plants name	Common Name	Reference no.
Abutilon indicum	Chakrabhenda	9182
Andrographis peniculata	Chiretta	9183
Allium cepa	Onion	9184
Phoenix dactylifera	Date palm	9185

Table showing plants names and authentication numbers

3. Processing and Extraction of plant materials

The plant materials washed with tap water and dried at 35-40°C for shed drying. After drying plant materials was grinded to make fine powder and stored in paper bags.

Extraction Materials:-

Extraction Methods:

A. *Phoenix dactylifera* (Fruits): About 100 gm. of *Phoenix dactylifera* fruits (without seeds) powder was extracted by 70% ethanol using soxhlet apparatus and was concentrated to dryness extract stored in freeze until use. (Tandon V. *et al.*, 2005).

B. *Andrographis peniculata* (Leaves): About 100 gm. of *Andrographis peniculata* leaves powdered and extracted with 70% ethanol using soxhlet apparatus and was concentrated to dryness. Both extract pooled and evaporated. Extract stored in freeze (Tandon V. *et al.*, 2005).

C. *Allium cepa* (Bulbs): About 100 gm. of *Allium cepa* (Bulbs) powder extracted with double distilled water (autoclaved) soxhlet apparatus and was concentrated to dryness and extract stored in freeze

D. *Abutilon indicum*. (Leaves and seeds): About 100 gm. of *Abutilon indicum* Leaves and seeds separately powdered and extracted with double distilled water (autoclaved) using soxhlet apparatus and was concentrated to dryness and extract stored in freeze.

4. Preliminary phytochemical screening for plant constituent

Phytochemical screening of active plant extracts was done by following the standard method of Khandelwal K.R. (2000), for the qualitative analysis of various studies such as alkaloids, coumarins, Saponins, flavonoides and steroids.

Reagents and chemicals:-

- **Mayer's reagent:** - 1.36 g of mercuric chloride was dissolved in 60 ml of distilled water and 5 g of potassium iodide in 20 ml of double distilled water. The solution were mixedand diluted to 100 ml with distilled water.
- **Wagner's reagent:**-Prepared by dissolving 1.27 g of iodine & 2 g of potassium iodide in100 ml double distilled water.
- Chloroform, Acetic anhydrite, 95% ethanol, dilute NaOH, conc.H_2SO_4, conc. HCL, and Mg++ crystals etc.

Methods of Tests:

A. Alkaloids

Mayer's Test: - Few drops of Mayer's reagent added to 2-3 ml test sample, creamy precipitate observed.

Wagner's Test: - Few drops of Wagner's reagent added to 2-3 ml test sample, reddish brown colour observed.

B. Coumarins

Aromatic odor: Coumarins give aromatic odor.

Filter Paper Test: Test sample taken in the test tube and covered with filter paper soaked in dilute NaOH and kept in hot water bath, after some time paper gives yellowish green fluorescence.

C. Saponins

Foam Test: Shaken the plant extracts vigorously with water, persistent foam observed.

Hemolytic Test: Add the sample to one drop of blood placed on glass slide. Hemolytic zones appeared.

D. Flavonides

Shinoda test: A small quantity of test residue dissolved in 5 ml ethanol (95%), treated with few drops of conc. HCL 0.5gm and Mg++ metals added, the pink crimson/ magenta colour developed with a minute or two.

E. Steroids

Salkowaski Reaction: 2ml test samples taken with chloroform and add 2 ml conc.H_2SO_4 shake the test tube. Chloroform layer appeared red and acid layer shows greenish yellow fluorescence.

Liberman-Bachard Reaction: 2 ml of the test sample taken with chloroform, add 1-2 ml acetic anhydride from the side of the test tube. First red, then blue and finally green colour appeared.

5. Isolation of strains of *Mycobacterium tuberculosis* from Patients.

The bacteria were isolated by using Petroffs Method and cultured on freshly prepared L.J Medium for pure culture as per WHO guidelines. The colonies obtained were sub cultured for pure colonies and referred as Patient's Isolated Strains (PIS) of *Mycobacterium tuberculosis*. The standard strain of *Mycobacterium tuberculosis* (SSM) i.e. H37Rv

Each PIS and SSM were sequentially diluted in normal saline up to the 10^3 bacteria/ml, 10^2 bacteria/mland were cultured on L.J Medium as prescribed by the in WHO manual for the lab testing. Each culture was tested for the positive for AFB Acid Fast Staining. The strains PIS and SSM were tested for the anti tubercle activity for plants extracts.

- **To Correlate and compare the anti tubercle activity between routine medicine and isolated plant extracts.**

The plants extracts and routine anti tubercle drugs were incorporated in the L.J. Medium before inspissation as per the WHO guidelines. The L.J. Medium were inoculated and incubated. Preparation of the media, bacterial suspensions and dilutions, inoculation of the media, incubation, reading schedule and reporting were those recommended for first line-drugs. Lowenstein-Jensen (L-J) without potato starch with drugs incorporated before inspissation was used. The modification of the International Union Against Tuberculosis (IUAT) is recommended (Jensen K. A, 1955, International Union Against Tuberculosis and Lung Disease, 1998). Screw-capped tubes 17 mm in diameter, containing 7 ml of medium are inspissated at 85°C during 40-45 minutes. L-J medium with and without incorporated drugs was stored at 4°C for one month. The indirect drug susceptibility test was carried out from a primary isolation or a sub-culture on LJ medium. A representative portion of the culture was obtained by sampling as many colonies as possible within 1 or 2 weeks after appearance of growth. The sample is homogenized in a sterile screw-capped bottle (e.g. 14 ml McCartney bottle or 5 ml Bijoux bottle) containing 1 ml H_2O and 10 glass beads 3.0 mm in diameter. The mixture was homogenized on a Vortex mixer for up to a minute and if needed the opacity is adjusted by the addition of sterile, distilled H_2O, down to that of a standard suspension of 1.0 mg/ml of BCG. The suspension was left to settle for about 30 minutes. Serial dilutions of 10^{-1} mg/ml to 10^{-5} mg/ml of the standard suspension were prepared by diluting sequentially 1.0 ml of the standard suspension (1 mg/ml) in tubes containing 9 ml of sterile distilled H_2O. Dilutions of 10^{-3} mg/ml and 10^{-5} mg/ml were inoculated on L-J and on drug/ extract containing L-J medium. For each isolate, two bacterial dilutions of the suspension are made; for each dilution of the suspension two control tubes are inoculated and one tube was inoculated for each drug and for each plant extracts concentration prepared. Therefore, for each drug and for each plant extract concentration 16 tubes have to be inoculated in total. The volume of the inoculum is 0.4 ml.

Quality control of medium batches

The test, carried out with the *Mycobacterium tuberculosis* reference strain H37Rv, consists in determining for each drug and each drug concentration used, the proportion of drug resistant bacilli in this strain.

As the proportion is very low, the quality control test differs slightly from the regular drug susceptibility test. The following dilutions of the standard bacterial suspension (1 mg/ml) are inoculated on a control tube and on a tube of each drug and extract concentration tested:

1)10^{-1}, 10^{-2}, 10^{-3} mg / ml

The following dilutions of the standard bacterial suspension (1 mg/ml) are inoculated on two control tubes:

10^{-5} and 10^{-6} mg / ml

The definitive reading of the test is done on the 28th and 40th day of incubation at 37° C. Colony counting and the calculation of proportions are carried out as in a regular drug susceptibility test. This test was carried out on each new batch of media.

7. To correlate Blood groups and its relation with tuberculosis

This study deals with freshly diagnosed sputum positive pulmonary tuberculosis cases on DOTS Therapy. Blood groups of all the above persons were determined by testing the individual's red blood cells with various antisera and by identifying antibodies in his own serum by testing against cells containing known antigens.

8. To study the relation between vitamin C and anti TB action of the plant extracts used

Estimate vitamin C from blood/plasma and also of various plant extracts were done by colorimetric method. (KYAW Method)

A. Materials and Reagents

i. Colour Reagent (Acid Phosphotungstate)

A. A mixture of 20gm of sodium tungstate [$Na_2No_4.H_2O$] and 10 gm of disodium hydrogen phosphate [$Na_2HPO_4.2H_2O$] was suspended in 30 ml of water and warm to dissolve.

B. To 15 ml of water 5 ml of H_2SO_4 (Gr 1.84) is added.

Solution B was poured slowly to solution A and the content was boiled gently for 2 hours under reflux [vigorous boiling should be avoided, since while pippeting may result on cooling] the resulting solution was then cooled to room temperature by allowing standing on bench. The solution is stable.

ii. Ascorbic Acid standard

A. Stock standard: - 50 mg/dl in 0.5% oxalic acid.

B. Working standard: - The stock was diluted 50 times for a working standard of 1 mg/dl with 0.5% oxalic acid. Oxalic Acid $C_2H_2O_4.2H_2O$ M.W. 126.07

In this method standard solutions were prepared at 10 µg/ml, 2 ml PTA added to each tube and plant extract/ plasma 2ml added to unknown. The blue colored supernatant taken out without disturbing precipitate and absorbance was read at 700 nm and final concentration of vit c was calculated.

9. Estimation of common serum enzymes observed in TB patients who were on routine chemotherapy of TB

Estimation of common serum enzymes in 100 tuberculosis patient was conducted in DOT center at Nagpur. All of them were receiving standard treatment for tuberculosis (Anti tuberculosis drugs). Detail history of each subjects were taken. According to category of treatment blood samples were collected and analysis was done with the help of Biochemistry auto analyzer. Analysis of Aspartate Amino Transferase (AST) and Alanine Amino Transferase (ALT) enzymes by Retimans and Frankel method (1957), while King and Wotton's method (1964) were used for Alkaline Phosphatase (ALP) analysis.

10. Comparative study of protein, albumin and protein / Albumin ratio in normal person, TB patient and TB with HIV patient

The study was carried out for serum protein, albumin and protein / albumin ratio determination in 100 tuberculosis patient, with selection of TB patient and TB with HIV patient. All of them were receiving DOTS treatment for tuberculosis. At the same time selection of normal subjects was done. Blood samples were collected with detail history of each subject was noted down. Sample analysis was done by using standard kit and standard method.

11. Statistical Analysis

Epi Info Software used for data analysis. Student's t- test was used for statistical analysis to compare the mean percentage of sample readings with respective controls. P values of < 0.05 were considered as significant.

CHAPTER SIX

Research Results

Table No. 06:- Percentage yields of Plant extracts.

No.	Name of Plants	Part Used	Percentage yields in gm (w/w)
1.	*Abutilon indicum*	Leaves	4.8
2.	*Abutilon indicum*	Seeds	5.4
3.	*Allium cepa*	Bulbs	6.3
4.	*Andrographis peniculata*	Leaves	6.7
5.	*Pheonix dactylifera*	Fruits	6.9

Table No. 07:- Showing the phytochemical components in plant extracts.

No	Plant phytochemical and testing methods	*Abutilon Indicum* Leaves	*Abutilon indicum* Seeds	*Andrographis peniculata*	*Allium cepa*	*Pheonix dactylifera*
1.	**Alkaloids**					
	Mayer's Test	+	+	-	+	+
	Wagner's Test	+	+	-	+	+
2.	**Coumarins**					
	Aromatic	-	-	+	+	-
	Odor	-	-	+	+	-
	Filter paper					
3	**Saponins**					

	Foam Test Hemolytic Test	+ +	+ +	+ +	+ +	+ +
4	**Flavonides** Shinoda Test	+	+	+	-	+
5	**Steroids** Salkowaski reaction Liberman Bucherd Reaction	+ +	+ +	- -	- -	- -

Table No. 08:- Showing proportion of resistant bacilli among standard strain H37Rv at bacterial dilutions of 100 bacteria/ml and extract/antibiotic conc. 200 µg/ml(SSM-100-200) (n=3, Mean ± S.D.)

S.No	Plant Extracts at conc.200 µg/ml	No of colonies obtained after 28th days of incubation Mean ± S.D.	Proportion of resistant bacilli
•	Control (plain culture)	18±1.0	--------
•	*Abutilon indicum* (Seed)	4.0 ± 0.70	0.022
•	*Abutilon indicum* (Leaves)	6.0 ± 1.58	0.333

Table 7 and 8

S.No	Plant Extracts at conc.200 µg/ml	No of colonies obtained after 28th days of incubation Mean ± S.D.	Proportion of resistant bacilli
•	Control	36.0 ± 2.0	--------
•	*Abutilon indicum* (Seed)	4.0 ± 0.70	0.011
•	*Abutilon indicum* (Leaves)	6.0 ± 1.58	0.166
•	*Andrographis peniculata*	1.0± 0.70	0.55
•	*Allium cepa*	0#	0#
•	*Pheonix dactylifera*	0#	0#
•	INH 200µg/ml	4.0 ± 0.70*	0.111
•	PZA 200µg/ml	5.0 ± 0.70*	0.138
•	RIF 200µg/ml	2.0 ± 0.70*	0.055
•	ETH 200µg/ml	1.0 ± 0.0*	0.0277

*Significant at level of $p<0.05$ when compared with respective control levels.

#No growth and hence no SD

(Statistical analysis was done by one-way ANOVA followed by Tukey's Multiple Comparison Test EPI info V3.3.2.)

INH-Isoniazide, RIF-Refampicine, PZA-Parazimide,

Table : Showing proportion of resistant bacilli among standard strain H37Rv at bacterial dilutions of 100 bacteria/ml and extract/antibiotic conc. 200 µg/ml(SSM-1000-200) (n=3, Mean ± S.D.)

Table No. 10:- Showing proportion of resistant bacilli among standard strain H37Rv at bacterial dilutions of 100 bacteria/ml and extract/antibiotic conc. 400 µg/ml (SSM-100-400) (n=3, Mean ± S.D.)

S. No.	Plant Extracts at conc.400 µg/ml	No of colonies obtained after 28th days of incubation Mean ± S.D.	Proportion of resistant bacilli
•	Control	18.0 ± 1.0	--------
•	*Abutilon indicum* (Seed)	8.0 ± 0.70*	0.044
•	*Abutilon indicum* (Leaves)	10.0 ± 1*	0.55
•	*Andrographis peniculata*	2.0 ± 0.70*	0.55
•	*Allium cepa*	2.0 ± 0.70*	0.111
•	*Pheonix dactylifera*	1.0 ± 0.70*	0.0625
•	INH 400µg/ml	5.0 ± 1.0*	0.277
•	PZA 400µg/ml	4.0 ± 0.70*	0.22
•	RIF 400µg/ml	3.0 ± 1.41*	0.166
•	ETH 400µg/ml	4.0 ± 1.0*	0.22

*Significant at level of $p<0.05$ when compared with respective control levels.

#No growth and hence no SD

Table 10

Table No. 11:- Showing proportion of resistant bacilli among standard strain H37Rv at bacterial dilutions of 1000 bacteria/ml and extract/antibiotic conc. 400 µg/ml (SSM-1000-400) (n=3, Mean ± S.D.)

S.No	Plant Extracts at conc.400 µg/ml	No of colonies obtained after 28th days of incubation Mean ± S.D.	Proportion of resistant bacilli
•	Control	36.0 ± 2.0	--------
•	*Abutilon indicum* (Seed)	10.0 ± 0.70*	0.29411
•	*Abutilon indicum* (Leaves)	5.0 ± 1.0*	0.147
•	*Andrographis peniculata*	2.0 ± 0.70*	0.0588

Table 11

S.No	Plant Extracts at conc.200 µg/ml	No of colonies obtained after 28th days of incubation Mean ± S.D.	Proportion of resistant bacilli
•	Control	36.0 ± 2.0	--------
•	*Abutilon indicum* (Seed)	10.0 ± 0.70*	0.29411
•	*Abutilon indicum* (Leaves)	5.0 ± 1.0*	0.147
•	*Andrographis peniculata*	2.0 ± 0.70*	0.0588
•	*Allium cepa*	2.0 ± 0.70*	0.0588
•	*Pheonix dactylifera*	1.0 ± 0.70*	0.0625
•	INH 400µg/ml	8.0 ± 0.70*	0.22
•	PZA 400µg/ml	11.0 ± 0.70*	0.305
•	RIF 400µg/ml	3.0 ± 1.41*	0.277
•	ETH 400µg/ml	4.0 ± 1.0*	0.111

*Significant at level of $p<0.05$ when compared with respective control levels.

#No growth and hence no SD

(Statistical analysis was done by one-way ANOVA followed by Tukey's Multiple Comparison Test EPI info V3.3.2.)

INH-Isoniazide, RIF-Refampicine, PZA-Parazimide,

ETH-Ethambutol, SSM- standard strain H37Rv

Table 12 : Showing proportion of resistant bacilli among standard strain H37Rv at bacterial dilutions of 1000 bacteria/ml and extract/antibiotic conc. 400 µg/ml (SSM-1000-400) (n=3, Mean ± S.D.)

Table No. 13:- Showing proportion of resistant bacilli among Patient Isolated Strain (PIS) at bacterial dilutions of 1000 bacteria/ml and extract/antibiotic conc. 200 µg/ml(PIS-1000-200) (n=3, Mean ± S.D.)

S.No	Plant Extracts at conc.200 µg/ml	No of colonies obtained after 28th days of incubation Mean ± S.D.	Proportion of resistant bacilli
•	Control	36.0 ± 2.0	--------
•	*Abutilon indicum* (Seed)	7.0 ± 1.58*	0.205
•	*Abutilon indicum* (Leaves)	3.0 ± 1.41*	0.0882
•	*Andrographis peniculata*	2.0 ± 0.70*	0.0588
•	*Allium cepa*	1.0 ± 0.70*	0.0294
•	*Pheonix dactylifera*	1.0 ± 0.70*	0.0625
•	INH 200µg/ml	8.0 ± 0.70*	0.222
•	PZA 200µg/ml	6.0 ± 0.70*	0.166
•	RIF 200µg/ml	4.0 ± 1.41*	0.111
•	ETH 200µg/ml	2.0 ± 1.0*	0.055

Table 13

Table No. 14:- Showing proportion of resistant bacilli among Patient Isolated Strain (PIS) at bacterial dilutions of 100 bacteria/ml and extract/antibiotic conc. 400 µg/ml(PIS-100-400) (n=3, Mean ± S.D.)

S.No	Plant Extracts at conc.400 µg/ml	No of colonies obtained after 28th days of incubation Mean ± S.D.	Proportion of resistant bacilli
•	Control	16.0 ± 0.67	--------
•	*Abutilon indicum* (Seed)	11.0 ± 0.70*	0.6875
•	*Abutilon indicum*(Leaves)	16.0 ± 0.70*	1.00
•	*Andrographis peniculata*	7.0 ± 1.58*	0.4375
•	*Allium cepa*	4.0 ± 1.0*	0.3636
•	*Pheonix dactylifera*	1.0 ± 0.70*	0.0625
•	INH 400µg/ml	11.0 ± 0.70*	0.6875
•	PZA 400µg/ml	9.0 ± 1.0*	0.5625
•	RIF 400µg/ml	5.0 ± 1.0*	0.3125
•	ETH 400µg/ml	3.0 ± 1.41*	0.1875

*Significant at level of $p<0.05$ when compared with respective control levels.
#No growth and hence no SD
(Statistical analysis was done by one-way ANOVA followed by Tukey's Multiple Comparison Test EPI info V3.3.2.)
INH-Isoniazide, RIF-Refampicine, PZA-Parazimide,
ETH-Ethambutol, SSM- standard strain H37Rv

Table 14

Table No. 15:- Showing proportion of resistant bacilli among Patient Isolated Strain (PIS) at bacterial dilutions of 1000 bacteria/ml and extract/antibiotic conc. 400 µg/ml (PIS-1000-400) (n=3, Mean ± S.D.)

S.No	Plant Extracts at conc.400 µg/ml	No of colonies obtained after 28th days of incubation Mean ± S.D.	Proportion of resistant bacilli
•	Control	16.0 ± 0.67	--------
•	*Abutilon indicum (Seed)*	10.0 ± 0.70	0.625
•	*Abutilon indicum (Leaves)*	5.0 ± 1.0	0.3125
•	*Andrographis peniculata*	2.0± 0.70	0.125
•	*Allium cepa*	2.0± 0.70	0.125
•	*Pheonix dactylifera*	3.0 ± 1.41	0.1875
•	INH 400µg/ml	12.0 ± 0.70	0.75
•	PZA 400µg/ml	10.0 ± 0.70	0.625
•	RIF 400µg/ml	8.0 ± 0.70	0.5
•	ETH 400µg/ml	5.0 ± 1.0	0.3125

*Significant at level of $p<0.05$ when compared with respective control levels.

#No growth and hence no SD

Table 15

Blood Groups	Tuberculosis Patients No in %	Tuberculosis with HIV Patients No in %	Total
A	49	04	53
B	11	01	12
AB	06	01	07
O	24	04	28

Table No.16:- Distribution of Blood Groups among Tuberculosis Patient and Tuberculosis with HIV patients (n=100).

Table No. 17:-Table showing the Vitamin C contents of the plant extracts used in the study

Standards and Tests	Conc. (µg/ml)
T1(*Allium cepa* –bulb)	6.36
T2(*Andrographis peniculata* –Leaves)	1.0
T3(*Abutilon indicum*-Leaves)	0.40
T4(*Pheonix dactylifera* –Fruit)	9.66
T5(*Abutilon indicum*-seeds)	0.93

Conc. - Concentrations

Table 17

Table No. 18:- Category wise comparative study of serum Protein fraction in Tuberculosis Patients and tuberculosis with HIV patient, normal person: Results shown are Mean ± S.D.

Sr. Protein Fraction	Cat I (A)	Cat II (B)	Cat III (C)	TB+HIV	T values		
					AB	AD	BC
Total Protein	6.2±0.26	5.7±0.46	6.7±0.46	5.4±0.30	18.9*	40.30*	30.7*
Albumin	3.2±0.24	2.6±0.14	3.7±0.24	2.3±0.26	43.1*	50.8*	78.1*
Globulin	3.0±0.22	3.0±0.22	2.9±0.39	3.0±0.20	0.00	0.00	4.4*
A:G Ratio	1.0±0.16	0.8±0.8	1.3±0.20	0.7±0.10	4.9*	30.18*	12.0*

* Significant (p value < 0.001)

(Statistical analysis was done by one-way ANOVA followed by Tukey's Multiple Comparison Test EPI info V3.3.2.)

Table 18

Table No. 19 A:- Changes in serum enzymes level in TB patient according to Category of Treatment. (n=100, Mean ± S.D)

Serum Enzymes	Category I A	Category II B	Category III C
AST (IU/L).	59.0 ± 2.20	73.2 ± 2.37	50.4 ± 1.52
ALT (IU/L)	80.5 ± 1.47	140.4 ± 5.05	50.1 ± 1.83
ALP (IU/L)	271.8± 1.72	342.1 ± 17.79	252.8 ± 1.82

Category I, Category II, Category III is the category of patients on DOTS treatment.

For t tests A B and C titled to the column in the table.

Table 19A

Table No. 19 B :- Changes in serum enzymes level in TB patient according to Category of Treatment.

Serum Enzymes	Category I A	Category II B	Category III C	t values		
				AB	AC	BC
AST	59.0±2.20	73.2±2.37	50.4±1.52	87.8*	64.3*	161.9*
ALT	80.5±1.47	140.4±5.05	50.1±1.83	227.7*	259.0*	336.2*
ALP	271.8±1.72	342.1±17.79	252.8±1.82	78.6*	151.7*	99.8*

*Significant (p value < 0.001)

Category I, Category II, Category III is the category of patients on DOTS treatment.

For t tests A B and C titled to the column in the table.

Table 19B

After the authentication and identification by the P.G.Departemnt of Botany, Nagpur University, Nagpur, the plant's parts were dried and extracted as per the standard procedure. The percent yield for *Abutilon indicum* (Leaves) obtained 4.8, *Abutilon indicum* (Seeds) 5.4, *Allium cepa* (bulb) 6.3, *Andrographis peniculata* (Leaves) 6.7 and *Pheonix dactylifera* (fruits) 6.9.

Preliminary phyto-chemical screening of three active plant extracts with significant anti tubercle activity was carried out (Results in table 07). *Pheonix dactylifera* (fruit) extracts exhibit positive for Mayer's and Wegner's Test for alkaloids, Foam test & Hemolytic Test for saponins and shinoda test for flavonoids. *Andrographis peniculata* (Leaves) shows positive reactions to foam test and hemolytic test for saponins and aromatic odor and filter paper test for coumarins and shinoda test for flavonides. *Allium cepa* (bulb) extracts shows the positive test for Mayer's and Wegner's Test for alkaloids, Foam test & Hemolytic Test for saponins and aromatic odor and filter paper test for coumarins. The phytochemical analysis suggests that the *Abutilon Indicum* Leaves and seeds contain alkaloids, saponins, flavonoids and steroids. *Andrographis peniculata* Leaves contains Coumarins, saponins, flavonoids while the *Allium cepa* Bulb has alkaloids, Coumarins and Saponins and *Pheonix dactylifera* Fruit contains Alkaloids, Saponins, Flavonoids and Steroids.

Efficacy of all plant extracts was evaluated on the basis of their anti-tubercular activity, where two different experimental sets were performed using 100 bacterial cells per ml and 1000 bacterial cells per ml. Both the sets were treated with plant extracts of 200µg/ml and 400µg/ml separately. Anti-tubercle activity in relation to the numbers of colonies appearing was observed after 28th days of incubation.

Results for the identification of proportion of resistant bacilli among standard strain H37Rv at bacterial dilutions of 100 bacteria/ml and extract/antibiotic conc.200µg/ml were depicted in table no.8 whereextracts of *Pheonix dactylifera* and *Allium cepa* was found to be most active as very less numbers of colonies (0) were observed as compared to control (18±1.0) in the Lowenstein Jensen medium, followed by the extracts of *Andrographis peniculata* (1.0± 0.70), *Abutilon indicum*-seed (4.0 ± 0.70) and *Abutilon indicum*-Leaves (6.0 ± 1.58). The proportion of resistant bacilli was found for *Abutilon indicum*-seed(0.022),*Abutilon indicum* (Leaves) (0.333) and *Andrographis peniculata*(0.55). The proportion of resistant bacilli obtained among the antibiotics were INH(0.22), PZA(0.277), RIF(0.111), ETH(0.05).

The counting of colonies grown on the different slants the calculation of the proportion of resistant bacilli by comparing counts on drug free and drug containing L-J medium, the matching of the calculated proportion with the critical proportion of the drug in question to determine if the proportion is higher (resistant strain) or lower (susceptible strain).Hence when the proportion is higher it indicates that the strain is resistant and if lower then susceptible.

Results for the identification of proportion of resistant bacilli among standard strain H37Rv at bacterial dilutions of 1000 bacteria/ml and extract/antibiotic conc. 200µg/ml were shown in table no.09 whereextracts of *Pheonix dactylifera* and *Allium cepa* was found to be most active as very less numbers of colonies (0) were observed as compared to control (36.0 ± 2.0) in the Lowenstein Jensen medium, followed by the extracts of *Andrographis peniculata* (1.0± 0.70), *Abutilon indicum*-seed (4.0 ± 0.70) and *Abutilon indicum*-Leaves (6.0 ± 1.58). The proportion of resistant bacilli was found for *Abutilon indicum*-seed(0.011),*Abutilon indicum* (Leaves) (0.166) and *Andrographis peniculata*(0.55). The proportion of resistant bacilli obtained among the antibiotics were INH (0.11), PZA(0.138), RIF(0.055), ETH(0.027).

Results for the identification of proportion of resistant bacilli among standard strain H37Rv at bacterial dilutions of 100 bacteria/ml and extract/antibiotic conc. 400µg/ml were shown in table no.10 whereextracts of *Pheonix dactylifera* was found to be most active as very less numbers of colonies (1.0± 0.70) were observed as compared to control (18.0 ± 1.0) in the Lowenstein Jensen medium, followed by the extracts of *Andrographis peniculata* (2.0± 0.70), *Allium cepa* (2.0± 0.70) *Abutilon indicum*-seed (8.0 ± 0.70) and *Abutilon indicum*-Leaves (10.0 ± 1). The proportion of resistant bacilli was found for *Pheonix dactylifera*(0.0625), *Allium cepa* (0.111), *Abutilon indicum*-seed(0.044),*Abutilon indicum* (Leaves) (0.55) and *Andrographis peniculata*(0.55). The proportion of resistant bacilli obtained among the antibiotics were INH (0.277), PZA(0.22), RIF(0.166), ETH(0.22).

Results for the identification of proportion of resistant bacilli among standard strain H37Rv at bacterial dilutions of 1000 bacteria/ml and extract/antibiotic conc. 400µg/ml were shown in table no.11 whereextracts of *Pheonix dactylifera* and was found to be most active as very less numbers of colonies (1.0± 0.70) were observed as compared to control (36.0 ± 2.0) in the Lowenstein Jensen medium, followed by the extracts of *Andrographis peniculata* (2.0± 0.70), *Allium cepa* (2.0± 0.70) *Abutilon indicum*-seed (10.0 ± 0.70) and *Abutilon indicum*-Leaves (5 ± 0.70). The proportion of resistant bacilli was found for *Pheonix dactylifera*(0.0625) *Abutilon indicum*-seed(0.294),*Abutilon indicum* (Leaves) (0.147) and *Andrographis peniculata*(0.588) *Allium cepa* (0.0588). The proportion of resistant bacilli obtained among the antibiotics were INH (0.11), PZA(0.138), RIF(0.055), ETH(0.027).

Results for the identification of proportion of resistant bacilli among Patient Isolated Strain (PIS) at bacterial dilutions of 100 bacteria/ml and extract/antibiotic conc. 400µg/ml were shown in table no.12 whereextracts of *Pheonix dactylifera* and was found to be most active as very less numbers of colonies (1.0± 0.70) were observed as compared to control (36.0 ± 2.0) in the Lowenstein Jensen medium, followed by the extracts of *Andrographis peniculata* (2.0± 0.70), *Allium cepa* (2.0± 0.70) *Abutilon indicum*-seed (10.0 ± 0.70) and *Abutilon indicum*-Leaves (5 ± 0.70). The proportion of resistant bacilli was found for *Pheonix dactylifera*(0.0625) *Abutilon indicum*-seed(0.294),*Abutilon indicum* (Leaves) (0.147) and *Andrographis peniculata*(0.0588) *Allium cepa* (0.0588). The proportion of resistant bacilli obtained among the antibiotics were INH (0.22), PZA(0.305), RIF(0.277), ETH(0.111).

Results for the identification of proportion of resistant bacilli among Patient Isolated Strain (PIS) at bacterial dilutions of 1000 bacteria/ml and extract/antibiotic conc. 200µg/ml were shown in table no.13 whereextracts of *Pheonix dactylifera* and was found to be most active as very less numbers of colonies (1.0± 0.70) were observed as compared to control (36.0 ± 2.0) in the Lowenstein Jensen medium, followed by the extracts of *Andrographis peniculata* (2.0± 0.70), *Allium cepa* (1.0± 0.70) *Abutilon indicum*-seed (7.58 ± 1.58) and *Abutilon indicum*-Leaves (3.0 ± 1.41). The proportion of resistant bacilli was found for *Pheonix dactylifera*(0.0625) *Abutilon indicum*-seed(0.205),*Abutilon indicum* (Leaves) (0.088) and *Andrographis peniculata*(0.0588) *Allium cepa* (0.0294). The proportion of resistant bacilli obtained among the antibiotics were INH (0.22), PZA(0.166), RIF(0.111), ETH(0.055).

Results for the identification of proportion of resistant bacilli among Patient Isolated Strain (PIS) at bacterial dilutions of 100 bacteria/ml and extract/antibiotic conc. 400µg/ml were shown in table no.14 whereextracts of *Pheonix dactylifera* and was found to be most active as very less numbers of colonies (1.0± 0.70) were observed as compared to control (16.0 ± 0.67) in the Lowenstein Jensen medium, followed by the extracts of *Andrographis peniculata* (7.0± 1.58), *Allium cepa* (4.0± 0.70) *Abutilon indicum*-seed (11 ± 0.70) and *Abutilon indicum*-Leaves (16.0 ± 0.70). The proportion of resistant bacilli was found for *Pheonix dactylifera* (0.0625) *Abutilon indicum*-seed (0.687), *Abutilon indicum* (Leaves) (1.0) and *Andrographis peniculata* (0.4375) *Allium cepa* (0.3636). The proportion of resistant bacilli obtained among the antibiotics were INH (0.6875), PZA(0.5625), RIF(0.3125), ETH(0.1875).

Results for the identification of proportion of resistant bacilli among Patient Isolated Strain (PIS) at bacterial dilutions of 1000 bacteria/ml and extract/antibiotic conc. 400µg/ml were shown in table no.15 whereextracts of *Andrographis peniculata, Allium cepa* and was found to be most active as very less numbers of colonies (2.0± 0.70)were observed as compared to control (16.0 ± 0.67) in the Lowenstein Jensen medium, followed by the extracts of *Pheonix dactylifera*(3.0 ± 1.41), *Abutilon indicum*-seed (10 ± 0.70) and *Abutilon indicum*-Leaves (5.0 ± 1.0). The proportion of resistant bacilli was found for *Pheonix dactylifera* (0.1875) *Abutilon indicum*-seed (0.625), *Abutilon indicum* (Leaves) (03125) and *Andrographis peniculata* (0.125) *Allium cepa* (0.125). The proportion of resistant bacilli obtained among the antibiotics were INH (0.75), PZA(0.625), RIF(0.5), ETH(0.3125).

As per the table no 16 the study of the prevalence of blood groups among the TB patients and TB+HIV patients shows that the 49% were of blood group A, 11% of blood group B, 06% of blood AB and 24 % belongs to blood group O.

The table no 17 shows that the *Pheonix dactylifera* has the concentration of 9.66µg/ml, and *Allium cepa* has 6.36 µg/ml of Vitamin C concentration, the *Andrographis peniculata, Abutilon indicum*-seed , *Abutilon indicum* (Leaves) were found to have 1.0 µg/ml, 0.93 µg/ml, 1.0 µg/ml respectively.

The serum protein fractions results are shown in table no.18. The whole blood samples from the TB patients of different category of treatment were collected for the estimation of Total proteins, albumin, globulin and A/G ratio. The total protein level was found on lower in cases of patients of category II and TB+HIV cases(5.7±0.46) and (5.4±0.30) respectively.

The results shown in table no 19 is of different serum enzymes of hepatic importance. The level of these enzymes Aspartate Amino Transaminase (AST), Alanine Amino Transaminase (ALT), and Alkaline Phosphatase (ALP) rises in case of hepatocellular damage. Increase values are observed in case of TB patients of category II.

Graph shown in Plate No. 18, the *Abutilon indicum* (Leaves) had least overall activity against the tubercle bacilli. Table 8 to table 10 showed the activities against the standard strain in various dilutions and it was observed from the graphical representation that extracts of *Pheonix dactylifera* was more active against the SSM as compared to PIS. In table no 8and 9 i.e. proportion of resistant bacilli among standard strain H37Rv at bacterial dilutions of 100 bacteria/ml and proportion of resistant bacilli among standard strain H37Rv at bacterial dilutions of 1000 bacteria/ml, *Andrographis peniculata* is simultaneously active like that of *Pheonix dactylifera* and thus can be an useful remedy for the future prospects of new development of medicines for tuberculosis.

Andrographis peniculata and *Pheonix dactylifera* (Fruits) were extracted in 70% ethanol, percentage yields 6.7gm and 6.9 gm (w/w) were calculated respectively. *Abutilon indicum* (Leaves), *Abutilon indicum* (Seeds), *Allium cepa* (Bulbs) extracted in double distilled water was found to be 4.8 gm, 5.4 gm, 6.3 gm (w/w) respectively.

The table No 16 shows total number of positive tuberculosis cases studied was 90 and tuberculosis with HIV Patients in this study was 10. This study deals with frequency distribution of A, B, AB, and O blood groups among tuberculosis patients as well as among freshly diagnosed tubercular with HIV positive cases. The results revealed that there was preponderance of group A and O, closely followed by group A and O among tubercular with HIV patients, exactly similar was the observation of other study. Such variations have been reported among different states of Indian Union. Preponderance of blood group B was reported also among Punjab (Talwar *et al*, 1958) and Bengalis (Sen *et al* 1959).But group O was more frequently observed among Kashmir's (Anand *et al*, 1963).

In the present study group A and group O was significantly more common among tuberculosis cases. The results revealed that there was same proportion in tuberculosis and tuberculosis with HIV positive patients. Regarding association of blood group and tuberculosis contradictory reports are available. No influence of blood group was observed by Mitra (1933) on diseases including tuberculosis except in helminthiasis and malignancy.

The maximum concentration of the Vitamin C was observed in the ethanolic extract of *Pheonix dactylifera* –Fruit (9.66µg/ml) and the lowest concentration of Vitamin C was observed in the aqueous extracts of Abutilon *indicum*-seeds and the other plants lie in between of the said two extracts with second most having high concentration of Vitamin C was *Allium cepa* –bulb(6.36 µg/ml). One gram of the extract was made soluble in 1 ml of demonized distilled water and then used as unknown in the said experiment by KWAY Method, hence the concentration of Vitamin C is solid powder form used was 9.66ug/gm and so on for all the extracts estimated for Vitamin C concentrations.

When studied for the anti tubercle activity the present study showed that the extracts having more Vitamin C content had more anti tubercle activity and vice versa.

Results found that serum protein fraction levels are decreased in category of treatment II as compare to category of treatment I and III. More decreased level found in tuberculosis with HIV patient as compare to tuberculosis patient in category of treatment II. Significant association was seen between category of treatment and tuberculosis with TB+HIV patient except globulin protein fraction.

In the present study serum protein determination was done in 90 tuberculosis patients, with selection of category of treatment. At the same time, with the determination of serum protein fractions in tuberculosis with HIV patients (30) and 30 normal healthy person, using same method. Table 18 shows results in Mean and Standard deviation among studied subjects. In tuberculosis cases study subjects were selected according to category of treatment I, category of treatment II and category of treatment III. All of them studied subjects were taking a treatment in DOT center. 30 patients were selected for each Category of treatment. 30 patients were taken from tuberculosis with HIV patient and 30 healthy subjects were selected for comparative study among them. Results found that serum protein fraction levels are decreased in category of treatment II as compare to category of treatment I and III. More decreased level found in tuberculosis with HIV patient as compare to tuberculosis patient in category of treatment II. Total protein values vary slightly in patients with tuberculosis. Hypoproteinemia occurs only in category of treatment II. Protein fraction changes according to the different stages of the disease. In tuberculosis category II there albumin mean value is 2.6 it is low as compare to category I and III. Study found that tuberculosis with HIV patients having too much low albumin level. Comparatively study among tuberculosis and tuberculosis with HIV patient shows serum protein fraction was low as compare to tuberculosis patient.

It was Adler' who in 1919 possibly for the first time carried out studies on the determination of serum proteins in patients sufferings from tuberculosis. He was followed by several investigators who, by means of different techniques achieved quite the same results.

Changes in serum enzymes level in TB patient (table 19) show significant increased mean level of enzymes could be seen in category II. The t values obtained in this table show significant difference between Categories I, II and III.

Table 19 shows Aspartate Amino Transferase (AST) and Alanine Amino Transferase (ALT) levels were determined by Retimans and Frankel method. Serum alkaline phosphatase was determined by King and Wotton's method (1964). The findings are set according to range and Mean & std. deviation of each serum enzymes. Table shows in category of Treatment I serum enzymes levels are slightly increased. The serum enzymes levels reached its maximum average value in the category of Treatment II. While in the category of Treatment III serum enzymes level returned to normal range. The overall incidence of raised serum enzymes level was greater in the patient of category of Treatment II.

CHAPTER SEVEN

Discussion and conclusion

Tuberculosis (TB) is an infectious disease of worldwide occurrence. Each year approximately 2 million person worldwide die off tuberculosis and 9 million become infected (Centers for disease control and prevention 2007).

In the United States, approximately 14000 cases of tuberculosis were reported in 2006, a 3.2 % decline from the previous year, 20 states and districts of Colombia had higher rates(Centers for disease control and prevention 2007).India is the highest TBburden countries in the world in 2008 nearly 2 million cases were reported in India and 2,76,000 persons die off this disease(World Health Organization, 2009). The prevalence of tuberculosis is continuing to increase because of patients affected with human immunodeficiency virus (HIV), bacterial resistance to medications (Goldrick BA, 2004). Manifestations of TB often include progressive fatigue, malaise, weight loss and low grade fever accompanied by chills and night sweat (TB elimination, online accessed January 28,2009).

Although the pulmonary system is the most common location for TB, extra-pulmonary disease occurring more than 20% of immuno-competent patients and risk for extra-pulmonary disease increase with immunosuppression (Surveillance reports, 2005). Although co-infection with human immunodeficiency virus (HIV) is the most notable cause for progressive to active disease, other factor such as uncontrolled diabetes mellitus, sepsis, renal failure, malnutrition smoking, chemotherapy, organ transplantation and long term corticosteroids usage that can trigger reactivation of remote infection are more common in critical care setting (Frieden TR *et al.*2003).

The drugs currently used to treat TB infection are mainly rifampicin, ethambutol, Isoniazide and pyrazinamide but the emergence of multiple drug resistant (MDR) strains of *M. tuberculosis* (defined resistance against Isoniazide and rifampicin)is now common in number of patients because of uncontrolled application of this anti tuberculosis drugs(Leonard MK *et al.* 2005). At present the more drug resistant form of tuberculosis XDR-TB (extensively drug resistant tuberculosis) has been reported such as current frontline drugs (isoniazid and rifampicin) in addition to any fluoroquinolone and at least one of the three injectable second line drugs (capreomycin, kanamycin, amikacin) (Raviglione MC,2006).

Tuberculosis is an infection caused by the rod shaped non spore forming aerobic bacterium *Mycobacterium tuberculosis* and is 0.5 µm to 3 µm long are classified as acid fast bacilli and have a unique cell wall structure crucial to their survival (Porth CM, 2002). The compositions in quantity of the cell wall components affect the bacteria's virulence and growth rate (Lee RB *et al.* 2005). The peptidoglycan polymer confers cell wall rigidity and it's just external to bacterial cell membrane, another contributor to the permeability barrier of *Mycobacteria* (Khare CP, 2007).

Another important component of the cell wall is lipoarabinomannan, a carbohydrate structural antigen on the outside of the organism that is immunogenic and facilitates the survival of *Mycobacteria* within macrophages (Joe M *et al.*2007)

The herbs proved to be hepato-protective in nature and showed anti-tubercle activity in comparison with the routine antibiotics. The herbal extracts have potential to be developed as alternative medicine for the antibiotics routinely used to treat tuberculosis. The routine antibiotics have side effects, long course of treatment and danger of development of drug resistance. Hence, after the discovery of anti-tubercle drugs mankind needs a new and effective medicine for tuberculosis. Herbal extracts have the potential to become an alternative for the anti-tubercle antibiotics.

Herbal extracts are usually a combination of several phytocompounds that synergistically act together. Typical pharmacological features of herbal preparations are metabolic activators, preventive agents against toxic effects, immunobalancing, immunomodulating, antioxidants, rejuvenating and energy boosting. All these features point toward their multi-variant nature and their pharmacological effects are due to the presence of many pharmacologically active ingredients that may affect more than a few genes. Very often, purified active components of herbal extract, if used alone, normally are not vary efficacious, however, combination of these components selectively and repeatedly interact with multiple sites and targets of a disease to achieve synergistic therapeutic responses (Bhatnagar and Gupta, 2011).

Unmet need, therefore, exists for highly effective and causality based treatments to which herbal pharmaceuticals are expected to contribute to a large extent. Moreover, natural herbal products offer unmatched structural variety too.

The efficacy of the selected plants was evaluated on the basis of proportion of resistant bacilli and different cell dilution as well as varying dose of herbal extracts against standard culture and culture isolated from the patients. It is well known fact that all the anti-tubercle medicines are potent hepato toxins and oblivious bring cellular enzymes into the blood stream. These enzymes are useful for the diagnosis of extent and type of hepato cellular damage caused by chemotherapy. Plant wise anti tubercle action is studied and found that the *Pheonix dactylifera* having the best anti-microbial activity against the PIS and SSM. The activity may be due to the presence of ample quantities of Alkaloids, Vitamin C, Saponins and Flavonoids. The data present in the tables 8-15 with focus on the calculation of the proportion of resistant bacilli. The proportion was found varying in herbal extracts and at lower side when compare with the routine antibiotics.

The best activities and corresponding concentrations of the plant extracts and the routine medicines are described in the coming discussion of the results.

The *Phoenix dactylifera, Allium cepa* shows maximum activity amongst all extracts/antibiotics against tubercle bacilli. At 400 ug/ml of the extract's concentration and at dilution of 1000 bacteria per ml *Allium cepa, Andrographis peniculata* shows maximum activity as compared to other and this is a finding that is useful for the development of new herbal drugs for tuberculosis as the routine chemotherapy available have several side effects and the said side effects are also responsible for the development of Multi-drug Resistant Tuberculosis (MDR-TB).

Fruit, bulb and leaves parts of *Abutilon indicum, Allium cepa Andrographis peniculata, Pheonix dactylifera* plants were taken and made extracts and counted the percentage of anti-tubercle activity and percentage yield. Different concentration of these plants extracts and different dilutions of different bacterial strains were taken and cultured together. The patient's isolated strains were isolated by Petroff's Method and cultured many times to get pure culture of the *Mycobacterium tuberculosis.* The culture of tubercle bacilli was done on Lowenstein Jensen medium. The routine antibiotics and the extracts of the parts of plants under study were incorporated aseptically during the preparation of Lowenstein Jensen medium. The extracts and the antibiotics were incorporated in definite concentrations of 200ug/ml and 400ug/ml. The *Mycobacterium tuberculosis* bacilli were pre-diluted to 100bacteria/ ml and 1000bacteria/ml ascetically and cultured on the Lowenstein Jensen medium with incorporated extracts and antibiotics in different concentrations.

In case of PIS (Patient Isolated Strain) it was also observed that the extracts of the *Andrographis peniculata* was more active as compared to that of the standard strain of tuberculosis. The antibiotics and the extracts were showing maximum activity at dilutions of 100 bacteria/ml. *Allium cepa* shows the maximum activity at 200 ug/ml of the extract's concentration and at dilution of 1000 bacteria per ml. The *Pheonix dactylifera, Allium cepa* shows maximum activity amongst all extracts/antibiotics against tubercle bacilli. Ethambutol was overall more active as compared with other antibiotics used in the study.

The extracts of *Pheonix dactylifera, Allium cepa, Andrographis peniculata* incomparison with Ethambutol, Refampicine and Isoniazide showed the maximum anti tubercle activity. Both the antibiotics and the extracts showed the maximum activity at dilutions of 100 bacteria/ml. *Andrographis peniculata* shows maximum activity at 400 ug/ ml of the extract's concentration and at dilution of 1000 bacteria per ml. In the review by Rajesh F. Udgirkar, *et al.*2012, anti-bacterial activity of *Abutilon indicum* was highlighted. Renu Gupta *et al.* in 2010 described that the

Abutilon indicum and *Allium cepa* along with *A. vasica, A. sativum* and *A. vera*exhibited activity against MDR isolates of *M. tuberculosis* in her research titled Anti-tuberculosis activity of selected medicinal plants against multi-drug resistant *Mycobacterium tuberculosis* isolates. This also supports the present study which undertaken before her work. Saha R, *et al.* in2011 mentioned that the *Allium cepa, Andrographis peniculata* and *Abutilon indicum* have anti-tubercle activity. The maximum activity against patient isolated strain of tuberculosis was found in the extracts of *Pheonix dactylifera, Allium cepa, Andrographis peniculata* incomparison with Ethambutol, Refampicine and Isoniazide. In case of PIS (Patient Isolated Strain) it was also observed that the extracts of the *Andrographis peniculata* was more active as compared to that of the standard strain of tuberculosis. The antibiotics and the extracts were showing maximum activity at dilutions of 100 bacteria/ml. *Allium cepa* shows the maximum activity at 200 ug/ml of the extract's concentration and at dilution of 1000 bacteria per ml. The *Pheonix dactylifera, Allium cepa* shows maximum activity amongst all extracts/antibiotics against tubercle bacilli. Ethambutol was overall more active as compared with other antibiotics used in the study. At 400 concentrations and 100 dilutions of bacilli the *Pheonix dactylifera* is most active in activity. When compared the 200-100(Concentration-bacterial dilution) and 200-1000 *Andrographis peniculata* was having the maximum % activity at this concentration of extracts and dilutions of bacilli respectively.

In the experiment for the anti-tubercle activity of routine chemotherapy for the tuberculosis it was observed that the Ethambutol was very active at bacterial dilutions of 100 and 1000 bacteria/ml for H37Rv strains and Parazimide and Isoniazide were showed to be having the least activity against both PIS and SSM of tubercle bacilli. Data from tables 12, 13, 14 and 15 suggests that the isolated strains from the patient were more resistant and when compared with the standard strains of bacilli it was noted that the over all resistance was increased in patient isolated strains as compared to standard strains and this is suggestive of more resistance in the patient isolated strains. Sivakumar A and Jayaraman G in 2011 in his the results shown that the anti tubercle activity of *Allium cepa*. Isoniazide was found active against standard strain at 400ug/ml and at bacterial dilution of 1000 bacteria/ml which was not found in case of patient isolated strain.

The possible underlying cause of anti-tubercle activity in *Pheonix dectylifera* may be due to the presence of the phytochemical like phenolics, sterols, carotenoids, anthocyanins, procyanidins and flavonoids. These phytochemicals also contribute to the nutritional and organoleptic properties of the fruits.(Ahmad Ateeq *et al.*2013).

The anti-tubercle activity observed in the extracts of *Allium cepa* may be due to the *Alliums* contain mainly cysteine sulfoxides, and when tissues are chopped, the enzyme allinase is released, converting the cysteine sulfoxides into the thiosulfinates. These compounds are reactive, volatile, odor producing and lachrymatory (Block *et al.* 1992). In addition to their nutritional effects, the antibacterial and antifungal activities against a variety of Gram-negative and Gram-positive were, and continue to be extensively investigated (Whitemore & Naidu, 2000). Han (1995) reported that the antibiotic activity of 1mg of allicin, which is a (+)-S-methyl-l-cysteine sulfoxide, has been equated to that of 15 IU of penicillin. Recent investigations have also demonstrated an inhibitory effect by aqueous extracts on numerous bacterial and fungal species (Sivam, Lampe, Ulness, Swanzy, & Potter, 1997; Phayet al., 1999; Hsieh, Mau, & Huang, 2001; Ward, Fasitsas, & Katz, 2002).

The present study also supports the anti-tubercle activity of Vitamin C. The study showed that the extracts of plant materials having higher concentration of Vitamin C have high anti tubercle activity as highest activity was observed in the extracts of *Pheonix dactylifera*(fruits) which had the 9.66ug/ml concentration of the Vitamin C when estimated by KYAW method, and the low anti tubercle activity was observed in the case of *Andrographis peniculata* –Leaves which had the 1.0 ug/ml concentration of vitamin C, the lowest concentration among all 5 plants used in the above study.

A person's individuality is antigens that are attached to surface of red blood cells and naturally occurring antibodies that circulate in the serum. The various combinations of their antigens and antibodies determine various blood groups. A proper correlation between blood groups and disease mechanism is required to be established as this study proves some correlation between the blood groups and development of disease. It may be suspected that blood group A might be having such immunological background that is very favorable for the infection of tubercle bacilli, but this may be changed from geographical region to region as one published work (Thamaria, J.P. *et.al)* stated that among general population of Northern part of Rajasthan there is a preponderance of blood group B, closely followed by O group.

O group was found significantly more frequent among sputum positive pulmonary tuberculosis cases than among general population. There seems to be no association between frequency distribution of blood groups and rate of inactivation of isoniazid among pulmonary tuberculosis cases. (Thamaria, J.P. *et.al*)

The frequency of blood groups varies in different races of the world (McCombs 1965). Such variations have been observed in different states of Indian Union (Talwar *et al.*, 1958; Sen *et al.*, 1959 and Anand *et al.*, 1963). There may be variation in frequency distribution of ABO group, in different parts of a state, e.g. Rajasthan. Jain (1968) has reported such frequency distribution among the population of Southern Rajasthan while data for Northern Rajasthan is not available and hence the present work on blood group estimation among TB patients was taken up. Blood group prevalence study has its important as a particular region has a trend of occurrence of tuberculosis infection in particular Blood Group.In the present study Blood Group A was found to be most affected when compared with the other blood group. One of the earliest attempts to find out an association between blood groups and disease was that of Buchanan and Hursley (1921-22) in a series of 2446 subjects wherein they concluded that there was no relationship between blood groups and any disease. Observations reported subsequently by various workers (Mitra, 1933 ; String & Rytias-quoted by Allan, 1955 ; Shenoy, 1962 and Jain, 1970), on the association of pulmonary tuberculosis and blood groups were contradictory. Therefore, it was decided to study this association again, particularly with reference to the rate of inactivation of Isoniazide, as both, rate of inactivation of INH and blood group of an individual are genetically controlled, a correlation between them may exist.

Estimation of blood groups was done among TB patient and Tuberculosis with HIV patients. Many previous study shows that there was no relationship between blood groups and any disease. Participated patients for this study are all in Vidharbha region. Following the estimation of blood group study found that blood group A is found more common in patients having pulmonary tuberculosis and blood group O is also found in some patients. According to findings, it may suspect that blood group A having such immunological background that is favorable of tubercle bacilli infection.

Infection induces a reduction in serum albumin and total protein level in human beings as well as experimental animals. In the present study the serum albumin and total proteins level were significantly reduced. The possible causes for the low albumin and total proteins in pulmonary tuberculosis patients were considered to be nutritional, enteropathy and acute phase reactant proteins (a. Karyadi,E *et al.*, 2000,b.Taneja,D.P,1990). The hepatic synthesis of phase reactant proteins is induced by cytokines such as interleukin-6 and tumor necrosis factor-α (Xing,Z.,1998,Gabay C1999).

The previous study showed that the infections induce a reduction in serum zinc and albumin levels in human beings and experimental animals. The possible causes of low serum zinc and albumin in Pulmonary Tuberculosis patients were considered to be the nutritional factors, enteropathy and acute phase reactant proteins.(Karayadi , 2000, Taneja,1990)

In this study, the results obtained as with reference to the table no 18 and it was observed that the lowest total serum proteins and albumins were observed in the tuberculosis with HIV infectious patients, category III patients serum proteins and albumin levels was very near to normal and suggestive of less impairment of liver due to the disease and/or due to side effects of chemotherapy. Albumin to globulin ratio is also observed lowest in cases of TB+HIV as compared to category I, category II, category III. Among category I, category II, category III the category II showed the lesser total serum proteins and serum albumins as compared to other two categories. As category II includes failure cases and relapse cases and they already had taken more doses of drugs and so they had more side effects from the routine chemotherapy for tuberculosis and this may be one of the causes for the lower total serum proteins and albumins levels. The study performed by Dr. Zia H. Khan and Shankar S. Warke in 2012, found that the Serum protein changes occurred because of anti-tuberculosis drugs. It was indicated that as the patients recovered there was a gradual significant decreased in Gamma globulin towards the normal value and after anti-tuberculosis treatment Albumin/Alpha-2 globulin gradually increases toward the normal levels on Six months Post treatment as improvement occurs.

The present study shows significantly lower levels of total protein and albumin in pulmonary tuberculosis patients. This agrees with Sasaki *et al.*(1999), who stated that albumin and total protein were significantly low in pulmonary tuberculosis. Aily *et al.* (1999) observed low levels of albumin and haematocrite in tuberculosis. Yamanaka *et al.* (2001) reported that the total protein, albumin, cholinesterase, hemoglobin and lymphocyte were significantly lower in homeless patients when compared with non-homeless tuberculosis patients and healthy men. Low levels of total protein and albumin in this study might have been caused by anorexia, malnutrition and mal-absorption commonly observed in tuberculosis. Albumin is an important component of plasma with antioxidant activity that primarily binds free fatty acids, divalent cations and hydrogen oxo-chloride (HOCI) (Llesuy *et al.*, 1994). The pro-oxidants (free radicals) attack the cell membrane thereby causing tissue damage and wasting disease in pulmonary tuberculosis patients with resultant high level of uric acid. The low level of albumin may therefore contribute to the complications associated with pulmonary tuberculosis. (Akiibinu M.O *et al.*2007).

The results were also revealed that serum protein fraction levels was decreased in category of treatment II as compared to category of treatment I and III. A further reduction was found in tuberculosis with HIV patient as compared to tuberculosis patient in category of treatment II. Total protein values vary slightly in patients with tuberculosis. Hypoproteinemia observed only in category of treatment II. Protein fraction changed according to the different stages of the disease. In tuberculosis category II there albumin mean value is 2.6 it is low as compare to category I and III. The final conclusion regarding protein study in the serum of tuberculosis patients supports the study as described above.

The hepatocellular damage caused by the routine antibiotics can be assessed by the estimation of the Enzymes of hepatic origin and same revealed that the category II Tb patients which includes relapse, failure in treatment patients are most severely affected by Hepatocellular damage due to long course of treatment and heavy dosage of antibiotics in combination. The raised levels of hepatic enzymes among the patients of tuberculosis taking DOTS treatment suggest that the category II patients were sufferer of hepatic injuries due the routine chemotherapy of tuberculosis. Category I is the second most affected category and the last one was category III. The study proves the patients of urban area of Nagpur Districts were sufferer of hepatic injuries due to medicines as side effect.

90 known cases of pulmonary tuberculosis were studied to assess the liver enzymes among them. They were getting treatment according to dots chemotherapy. On initiation of the treatment they were confirmed negative for HBsAg, anti-HCVAB and HIV. When study subjects in intensive phase among category of treatment I that period serum sample were collected and estimated. Same collection and estimation were done among of the next category. It was concluded that more chances of hepatic damage during tuberculosis regimen in category of treatment II. Study results found there were no risk in category of treatment III cause of these rise enzymes level come to near normal range.

Final conclusion supports that the new herbal drugs can be invented by the extracts of *Abutilon indicum, Allium cepa Andrographis peniculata, Pheonix dactylifera* by using various parts of the said plants. More in-depth research and analysis will be future need for exploring the anti-tubercle activity of the *Allium cepa Andrographis peniculata, Pheonix dactylifera* which showed good activity in the present study. As blood group A and O were observed more prone for the said disease the underlying cause can be studied in detail. As the overall serum proteins were decreased in the TB patient's protein supplements must be provided to patients on DOTS with routine medicines so that fast recovery will take place and chances of MDR-TB will get reduced.

CHAPTER EIGHT

Publications

Research Activities and publications done in the Research Study period:-

I) The following papers were published during the research study period:-

- Activity of Indian habitat plants extracts against *Mycobacterium tuberculosis* to treat tuberculosis. Biosciences, Biotechnology Research Asia, Vol.5 (1), 455-459(2008).

  S.C.Narwadiya,S.V.Saoji,U.L.Dhumne,P.M.Tumane,and V.G.Meshram.

- Assessment of liver enzymes level in the serum of tuberculosis patients during directly observed Short term chemotherapy (DOTS). Biomedical & Pharmacology Journal, Vol.1(2),449-452(2008). S.C.Narwadiya,,U.L.Dhumne,P.M.Tumane,and V.G.Meshram.

II) The following posters (topic summarized below) were presented during the research study period:-

- Relation of Tuberculosis with Blood Groups. Biotech Conference, 21st December 2006.
- Occurrence of Enzyme level changes in TB Patients after chemotherapy. National conference Biochem-2007 at PGDT of Biochemistry, RTM Nagpur University, Nagpur.27-29 December 2007.
- Activity against *Mycobacterium tuberculosis* of plant extracts from Indian habitat to treat tuberculosis. National conference Biochem-2007 at PGDT of Biochemistry, RTM Nagpur University, Nagpur. 27-29 December 2007.
- **Life Membership of Global Biotech Forum in November 2007.**
- **Trainings Attended :-**
- Proficiency in Basic DNA Techniques at Hi Media Laboratory Pvt Ltd, Mumbai.1-6th April 2008.
- FTIR Spectroscopic Analysis of Coal, Mineral and Free Silica at ISM Dhanbad during 01-05th December 2008.
- Quantitative Analysis for Empirical Research at Jawaharlal Nehru Aluminum Development and Design Centre (JNARDDC), Nagpur during 21-23 January 2009.

CHAPTER NINE

References

1. Abate G, Mshana, RN, Miörner H. 1998 : Evaluation of a colorimetric assay based on 3-(4,5-dimethyl-2-yl)-2,5-diphenyl tetrazolium bromide for rapid detection of rifampicin resistance in Mycobacterium tuberculosis. *Int J Tuberc Lung Dis* 2:1011–1016
2. Abdulla Y, Al–Taher. 2008: Possible anti-diarrhoeal effect of the date palm (*Phoenix Dactylifera L*) spathe aqueous extract in rats. Scientific Journal of King Faisal University (Basic and Applied Sciences). 9: 1429-1435.
3. Aboltins CA, Page MA, Buising KL, *et al.* 2007: "Treatment of staphylococcal prosthetic joint infections with debridement, prosthesis retention and oral rifampicin and fusidic acid". *Clinical Microbiology and Infection* 13 (6): 586–591
4. Abutilon_indicum,http://en.wikipedia.org/wiki/Abutilon_indicum[online] accessed on 19-05-2014
5. Adisakwattana S., K. Pudhom and S. Yibchok-anun 2009: Influence of the methanolic extract from *Abutilon indicum* leaves in normal and streptozotocin-induced diabetic rats African Journal of Biotechnology Vol. 8 (10), pp. 2011-2015, 18 May.
6. Ahmad Ateeq, Soni Dutta Sunil, Singh K Varun, Maurya K Santosh, 2013 *Phoenix dectylifera* Linn.(PIND KHAJURA): A REVIEW., *Int J Ayurveda Pharm* 4(3), May-June 2013
7. Ahmed M, Amin S, Islam M, Takahashi M, Okuyama E, Hossain CF. 2000:Analgesic principle from Abutilon indicum. Pharmazie. Apr; 55(4):314-316.
8. Aily DC, Camargo SS, Paro HS, Passos CA, Sato DN, Shikama M, Silva RR, Ueki SY. 1999: Systemic mycobacterioses in AIDS patients as determined by blood cultures on biphasic medium. *Revista Argentina de Microbiologia* 31(2):53-57.
9. Aird, I., Bentall, H.H. and Fraser Roberts, J.A.1953: Brit. Med. Jour,1, 79
10. Aird, I., Bentall, H.H., Mehigan, J.A. and Fraser Roberts, J.A. 1954: Ibid, 2, 315.
11. Akiibinu M.O, Arinola O.G, Ogunlewe J.O, and Onih E.A. 2007: Non-Enzymatic Antioxidants and Nutritional Profiles in Newly Diagnosed Pulmonary Tuberculosis Patients in Nigeria. *African Journal of Biomedical Research*, 10; 223 – 228.
12. Al farsi M, Alasalvar C, Morris A, Baron M, Shahidi F. 2005: Comparison of antioxidant activity, anthocyanins, carotenoids, and phenolics of three native fresh and sun dried date (*Phoenix dectylefera L.*) varieties grown in Oman. J Agric Food Chem 53;7592-7599.
13. Allaith, Abdul AA In vitro evaluation of antioxidant activity of different extracts of *Phoenix Dactylifera* L. fruits as functional foods. Deutsche Lebensmittel Rundschau. 2005; 101: 305-308.
14. Al-Miaman SA 2005: Effect of date palm (*Phoenix dectylefera*) seed fibres on plasma lipids in rats. J king Saud Univ. 17:117-123.
15. Al-Qarawi A, Abdel-Rahman H, Ali BH, Mousa HM, El-Mougy SA 2005: The ameliorative effect of dates (*Phoenix Dactylifera* L.) on ethanol-induced gastric ulcer in rats. J. Ethnopharmacol. 98: 313-317.
16. Al-Qarawi AA, Abdel-Rahman H., Mousa HM, BH Ali, El-Mougy SA 2008: Nephroprotective action of Phoenix dactylifera. in gentamicin-induced nephrotoxicity Pharmaceutical Biology 4: 227-230
17. Al-Qarawi AA, Ali BH, Al-Mougy SA, Mousa HM 2003: Gastrointestinal transit in mice treated with various extracts of date (*Phoenix Dactylifera* L.). Food and Chemical Toxicology 41:37–39.

18. Al-Qarawi AA, Mousa HM, Ali BEH, Abdel-Rahman H, El-Mougy SA. 2004: Protective effect of extracts from Dates (*Phoenix Dactylifera* L.) on carbon tetrachloride–induced hepatotoxicity in rats. Intern J Appl Res Vet Med; 2: 176-180,
19. Al-Shahib, W. and Marshall, R. J. 1993 : The fruit of the date palm: its possible use as the best food for the future *Int. J. Food Sci. Nut.* 54: 247-259.
20. Alteri *et al.*, Proc National Academy of Science, U S A. 2007 March 20;104(12): 5145–5150
21. American Thoracic Society 2003 CDC; Infectious Diseases Society of America. (Jun 20, 2003). "Treatment of tuberculosis." *MMWR Recomm Rep* 52 ((RR-11)): 1–77
22. American Thoracic Society Documents (2006) An Official ATS Statement: Hepatotoxicity of Anti-tuberculosis Therapy Jussi J. Saukkonen, David L. Cohn, Robert M. Jasmer, Steven Schenker, John A. Jereb, Charles M. Nolan, Charles A. Peloquin, Fred M. Gordin, David Nunes, Dorothy B. Strader, John Bernardo, Raman Venkataramanan, and Timothy R. Sterling, on behalf of the ATS Hepatotoxicity of Antituberculosis Therapy Subcommittee [online] accessed on 25-05-2014.
23. Anil Kumar, Jyotsna Dora, Anup Singh and Rishikant Tripathi 2012: A review of king of bitter (Kalmegh) *International Journal of research in Pharmacy and hemistry 2(1) 116-124.*
24. Anti-tubercle drugs http://en.wikipedia.org/wiki/Isoniazid[online] accessed on 18-05- 2014
25. Anti-tubercle drugs http://en.wikipedia.org/wiki/Pyrazinamide[online] accessed on 18-05-2014
26. Anti-tubercle drugs http://en.wikipedia.org/wiki/Streptomycin[online] accessed on 18-05-2014
27. Ashok Kumar Bagepalli Srinivasa, Lakshman Kuruba, , Saleemulla Khan, Gopi Setty Saran 2013: Antiurolithiatic Activity of Gokhsuradi Churan, an Ayurvedic Formulation By *In Vitro* Method. *Advanced Pharmaceutical Bulletin,* 3(2), 477-479
28. Ayesha Mateen , Suresh P.V.K., Parwez Ahmed 2007: Evalution of antibacterial activity of cuscuta reflexa and *Abutilon indicum* Journal of Medical Microbiology 56, 360–364
29. Bahmanpour S, Talaei T, Vojdani Z, Panjehshahin MR,. Poostpasand LA, Zareei S, Ghaeminia M. 2006 : Effect of *Phoenix Dactylifera* pollen on sperm parameters and reproductive system of adult male rats. IJMS; 31; 4.
30. Baladrin,M.F Klocke, JA, Wurtele, E.S and Bollingeer,W.H. 1985: Natural plant chemicals; *Sources of Industrial and Medicinal Materials Sciences*, 228,1154- 1160.
31. Batkhuu, J, Hattori, K, Takano, F, Fushiya, S, Oshiman, K, & Fujimiya, Y. 2002: Suppression of NO production in activated macrophages in vitro and ex vivo by neoandrographolide isolated from *Andrographis paniculata*. Biol Pharm Bull. 25(9), 1169-74.
32. Bemer P, Palicova FR, Rusch-Gerdes S, Drugeon HB, Pfyffer GE. 2002: Multicenter evaluation of fully automated BACTEC Mycobacteria Growth Indicator Tube 960 system for susceptibility testing of Mycobacterium tuberculosis. *J Clin Microbiol* 40:150–154.
33. Benkeblia 2004: Antimicrobial activity of essential oil extracts of various onions (*Allium N. cepa*) and garlic (*Allium sativum*) Lebensm.-Wiss. u.-Technol. 37 263–268
34. Benkeblia N. 2004: ntimicrobial activity of essential oil extracts of various onions (*Allium cepa*) and garlic (*Allium sativum*) Lebensm.-Wiss. u.-Technol. 37 263–268
35. Bhatnagar P, Gupta S, (2011), Herbal Drugs-Potent Promise, Biotech News, vol.6, No.4-6.
36. Block, E., Naganathan, S., Putman, D., & Zhao, S. H. 1992. *Allium* chemistry: HPLC analysis of thiosulfonates from onion, garlic, wild garlic, leek, scallion, shallot, elephant garlic, and Chinese chive. Uniquely high allyl to methyl ratios in some garlic samples. *Journal of Agriculture and Food Chemistry*, 40, 2418–2430.
37. Bokhari NA, Parveen K. 2005: In vitro inhibition potential of (*Phoenix dectylefera L.*) varieties growth in Oman. J agric food chem. 53:7586-7591.
38. Brewster, James L. 1994 Onions and other vegetable Alliums (1st ed.). Wallingford, UK: CAB International. p. 16. ISBN 0-85198-753-2.
39. Brickell, Christopher (ed) 1992: *The Royal Horticultural Society Encyclopedia of Gardening*. Dorling Kindersley. p. 345.

40. British Thoracic Society (1984). "A controlled trial of 6 months chemotherapy in pulmonary tuberculosis, final report: results during the 36 months after the end of chemotherapy and beyond". *Br J Dis Chest* 78 (4): 330–336
41. Calvori, C., Frontali, L., Leoni, L. and Tecce, G. (1965) Effect Ofrifamycin on Protein Synthesis. *Nature*, 207, 417-418. http://dx.doi.org/10.1038/207417a0
42. Calvori, C.; Frontali, L.; Leoni, L.; Tecce, G. 1965. "Effect of rifamycin on protein synthesis". *Nature* 207 (995): 417–8
43. Campbell, E.A., Korzheva, N., Mustaev, A., Murakami, K., Nair, S., Goldfarb, A., Darst, S.A. 2001: "Structural mechanism for rifampicin inhibition of bacterial RNA polymerase". *Cell* 104 (6): 901–12
44. Canetti G, Fox W, Khomenko A, 1969: Advances in techniques of testing mycobacterial drug sensitivity, and the use of sensitivity tests in tuberculosis control programmes. *Bull World Health Organ* 41:21–43.
45. Casenghi M. 2006: Development of new drugs for TB chemotherapy: Analysis of the current drug pipeline. *Médecins Sans Frontiéres.*
46. Center for disease control and prevention. Trends in tuberculosis incidence MMWR Morb Mortal wkly Rep 2007: 56(11) 245-250.
47. Chan, E.W.C., Lim, Y.Y., & Chew, Y.L. 2007: Antioxidant activity of Camellia sinensis leaves and tea from a lowland plantation in Malaysia. Food chemistry, 102(4), 1214-1222.
48. Charity JC, Katz E, Moss B, March 2007: "Amino acid substitutions at multiple sites within the vaccinia virus D13 scaffold protein confer resistance to rifampicin". *Virology* 359 (1): 227–32.
49. Chitra Shenoy, MB Patil, Ravi Kumar Swati Patil , 2009: Preliminary phytochemical investigation and wound healing activity of Allium Cepa Linn (Liliacae). International Journal of Pharmacy and Pharmaceutical Sciences, 2, Issue 2, July-Sep 167-175
50. Collins, R Douglas 1985: Atlas of Drug Reactions. New York, NY: ChurchillLivingstone pp. 123.
51. Copley M.S., Rose P.J., Clampham A., Edwards D.N.,Horton M.C. and Evershed R.P., 2001: Detection of palm fruit lipids in archaeological pottery from Qasr Ibrim, Egyptian Nubia, Proceedings of the Royal Society, London, 268,593–597.
52. Corbett, E.L, *et al.*2003: The growing burden of tuberculosis: Global trends and interactions with HIV epidemic. *Arch. Intern. Med.*163,1009-1021.
53. Culliton BJ 1992: Drug-resistant TB may bring epidemic. Nature 356 : 473.
54. Dammak I, Abdallah FB, Boudaya S, Besbes S, Keskes L, El Gaied A, Turki H, Attia H, Hentati B. 2007: Date seed oil limit oxidative injuries induced by hydrogen peroxide in human skin organ culture, 2007 Biofactors.29(2-3):137-45. PMID: 17673830
55. Dashputre N. L., N. S. Naikwade 2010: Immunomodulatory Activity of *Abutilon indicum* linn on Albino Mice International Journal of Pharma Sciences and Research (IJPSR) (3), 178-184.
56. Devaki V, Mohan K, Gangadharam PRJ 1969: Direct sensitivity test for isoniazid. *Indian J Med Res* 57 : 1006-10.
57. Diaz-Infantes MS, Ruiz-Serrano MJ, Martinez-Sanchez L, 1989: Evaluation of the MB/BacT mycobacterium detection system for susceptibility testing of *Mycobacterium tuberculosis. J Clin Microbiol* (2000) 38:1988–1989.
58. Drowart A, Cambiaso CL, Huygen K, *et al.* 1997: Detection of rifampicin and isoniazid resistance of *Mycobacterium tuberculosis* strains by particle counting immunoassay. *Int J Tuberc Lung Dis* 1:284–288.
59. drug regimen for tb, http://www.tbcindia.org/pdfs/TB-India-2008.pdf [online]accesses on 24-05-2014
60. Dye C, Watt CJ, Bleed DM *et al.*2005: Evolution of tuberculosis control and prospects for reducing tuberculosis incidence, prevalence, and deaths globally. *JAMA* 293: 2767-2775.
61. Dye C, Williams BG, Espinal MA, Raviglione MC 2002: Erasing the World's slow stain : strategies to beat multi-drugresistant tuberculosis. *Science* 295 : 2042-6.
62. El Hadrami, I. and A. El Hadrami. 2009: Breeding date palm. pp. 191-216. In: Jain S.M. and P.M. Priyadarshan (Eds.) Breeding Plantation Tree Crops, Springer, New York.
63. El-Desoky GE, Ragab AA, Ismail SA, Kamal AE. 1995: "Effect of palm-pollen grains (*Phoenix dactylifera*) on sexhormones, proteins, lipids and liver functions." J. Agric. Sci.Mansoura Univ. 20: 4249-4268.

64. Elgasim EA, Alyousif YA, Homeida AM: 1995: Possible hormonal activity of date pits and fleshfed to meat animals. Food Chem. 52: 149–150.
65. Erlich, Henry, W Ford Doolittle, Volker Neuhoff 1973 Molecular Biology of Rifomycin. New York, NY: MSS Information Corporation, pp. 44-45, 66-75, 124-130.
66. Erlich, Henry, W Ford Doolittle, Volker Neuhoff, and *et al.* 1973 Molecular Biology of Rifomycin. New York, NY: MSS Information Corporation, pp. 44-45, 66-75, 124-130.
67. Eswar Kumar K., K.N. Harsha, V. Sudheer, Nelli Giri babu, 2013: In vitro antioxidant activity and in vivo hepatoprotective activity of aqueous extract of Allium cepa bulb in ethanol induced liver damage in Wistar rats, food science and human wellness2, 132-138.
68. Ethambutol http://commons.wikimedia.org/wiki/File:strukturformel_mit Stereochemie. png[online] accessed on 19-05-2014
69. Extensively_drug-resistant_tuberculosis[online]http://en.wikipedia.org/ wiki/Extensively_drug-resistant_tuberculosis,accessed on 01-06-2014
70. F. Zuhre Badak, Servet Goksel, Ruchan Sertoz, Asuman Guzelant, Ahmet Kizirgil and Altinay Bilgic (1999) Cord Formation in MB/BacT Medium Is a Reliable Criterion for Presumptive Identification of *Mycobacterium tuberculosis* Complex in Laboratories with High Prevalence of *M. tuberculosis* J. Clin. Microbiol. , 37(12):4189.
71. Fatmah H., 2013: Effect of temph dates biscuits on nutritional status of preschool children with tuberculosis. Mal. J. Nutr 19(2) 173-184.
72. Feklistov, A., Mekler, V., Jiang, Q., Westblade, L.F., Irschik, H., Jansen, R., Mustaev, A., Darst, S.A., Ebright, R.H. 2008: "Rifamycins do not function by allosteric modulation of binding of Mg2+ to the RNA polymerase active center". *Proc Natl Acad Sci USA* 105 (39): 14820–5.
73. Fenton, M.J, Macrophages and tuberculosis *Curr. Opin. Hematol. 1998:* 1.72-78.
74. Fenton, M.J 1998: Macrophages and tuberculosis *Curr. Opin. Hematol.* 1.72-78.
75. Fransworth,N.R. 1998: Screening plants for new medicines In : Wilson, E.O.(Ed.), *Biodiversity, National Academic Press*, Washington, DC, 83-97.
76. Frieden TR, Sterling TR, Munsiff SS, Watt CJ, Dye C. Tuberculosis Lancet 2003; 362: 887-889.
77. G Curci, A Ninni, A.D'Aleccio 1969 Atti Tavola Rotonda Rifampicina, Taormina, page 19. Edizioni Rassegna Medica, Lepetit, Milano.
78. Gabay C, Kushner I, Acute-phase proteins and other systemic responses to inflammation, N Engl J Med. 1999 Feb 11;340(6):448-54
79. Gali N, Dominguez J, Blanco S, *et al.* 2003*:* Utility of an in-house mycobacteriophage-based assay for rapid detection of rifampicin resistance in *Mycobacterium tuberculosis* clinical isolates. *J Clin Microbiol* 41:2647–2649.
80. Ganga Rao B, Venkateswara Rao Y, Mallikarjuna Rao T, 2012: Hepatoprotective activity of *Spillanthes acmella* Extracts against CCl4-induced liver toxicity in rats. Asian Pacific Journal of Tropical Disease, 208-211.
81. Girling DJ. The hepatic toxicity of antituberculosis regimens containing isoniazid, rifampicin and pyrazinamide. Tubercle, 1978; 59: 13-32
82. Goldrick BA. Once Dismissed, Still rampant: tuberculosis, the second Deadliest infectious Disease worldwide. Am J Nurs 2004: 104(9): 68-70.
83. Gu, L.; Kelm, M. A.; Hammerstone, J. F.; Beecher, G.;Holden, J.; Haytowitz, D. and Prior, R. L. 2003: Screening of foods containing proanthocyanidins and their structural characterization using LCMS/ MS and thiolytic degradation. J. Agric. Food Chem, 51: 7513-7521
84. Guidelines for surveillance of drug resistance in tuberculosis. Geneva. *WHO/TB/96.216. 1997,*
85. Guno Sindhu Chakraborthy, Prashant M Ghorpade Antinociceptive Activity OF *Abutilon indicum* (Linn) Sweet Stem Extracts Arch Pharm Sci & Res Vol 2 No 1 241 - 245 January 2010
86. H.A. Abdelrahman, S.I. Fathalla,A.A. Mohamed, H.K. Jun and D.H. Kim 2012: Protective Effect of Dates (*Phoenix Dactylifera L.*) And Licorice (*Glycyrrhiza glabra*) on Carbon Tetrachloride-Induced Hepatotoxicity in Dogs, Global Veterineria 9(2):184-191.

87. H.Panda, Herb cultivation and medicinal uses, *National Institute of Industrial Publication devision*, New Delhi, pg.101.pg.125
88. Hager, Thomas: *The Demon Under the Microscope: From Battlefield Hospitals to Nazi Labs, One Doctor's Heroic Search for the World's First Miracle Drug*. Harmony Books 2006. ISBN 1-4000-8214-5
89. Han, J., Lawson, L., Han, G., & Han, P. 1995. A spectrophotometric method for quantitative determination of allicin and total garlic thiosulfinates. *Annals of Biochemistry*, 225, 157–160.
90. Hans L Riede 2009: "Fourth-generation fluoroquinolones in tuberculosis". *Lancet* 373 (9670): 1148–1149
91. Hawkins JE, Wallace RJ Jr, Brown BA. 1991: Antibacterial drug susceptibility tests: mycobacteria. In: Balows A, Hausler WJ, Herrmann KL, Isenberg HD, Shadommy HJ, eds. *Manual of clinical microbiology. 5th Edn. Washington DC*, American Society for Microbiology, pp. 1138–1152.
92. history of tuberculosis, http://en.wikipedia.org/ wiki / History _ of _ tuberculosis [online] accessed on 20-05-2014
93. http://altmedrev.com/publications/16/1/66.pdf [online] accessed on 24-05-2014
94. http://drbcshah.com/tuberculosis-tb/ Antibiotic resistant tb [online] accessed on 31-05-2014
95. http://en.wikipedia.org/wiki/Onion[online] accessed on 19-05-2014
96. http://en.wikipedia.org/wiki/Rifampicin[online]accessed on 18-05-2014
97. http://encyclopedia2.thefreedictionary.com/cord+factor[online], accessed on 10-05-2014
98. http://encyclopedia2.thefreedictionary.com/cord+factor[online]accessed on 18-05-2014
99. http://ispub.com/IJPHARM/7/1/8733[online]accessed on 24-05-2014
100. http://onions-usa.org/all-about-onions/onion-health-research[online] accessed on 20-05-2014
101. http://shelf3d.com/i/pyrazinamide[online]accessed on 18-05-2014
102. http://www.cdc.gov/nchstp/tb/notes/TBN_1_00/TBN2000Ruggiero.htm[online]accessed on 19-05-2014
103. http://www.docstoc.com/docs/27038162/Tuberculosis-and-Mycobacteria - Cell-Wall[online] accessed on 14-05-2014
104. http://www.globinmed.com/index.php?option=com_content&view=article&id=83494:abutilon-indicum&catid=199:safety-of-herbal&Itemid=139 [online] accessed on 19-05-2014
105. http://www.itis.gov/servlet/SingleRpt/SingleRpt?search_topic=TSN&search_value=184881[online] accessed on 24-05-2014
106. http://www.tbcindia.org/pdfs/TB-India-2008.pdf
107. http://www.who.int/tb/publications/global_report/2009/pdf/full_report.pdf#[online] accessed on 20-05-2014
108. http://www.who.int/tb/xdr/xdrtb_sept06news.pdf#[online] accessed on 20-05-2014
109. https://plants.usda.gov/core/profile?symbol=PHDA 4# [online] accessed on 20-05-2014
110. Hubert Bloch, 1949: Studies on the virulence of tubercle bacilli isolation and biological properties of a constituent O:F virulent organisms, October 14, The journal of experimental medicine 91,Plate12
111. I Azuma, H Kimura and Y Yamamura, 1968: Chemical and immunological properties of polysaccharides of wax D extracted from *Mycobacterium tuberculosis* strain from Aoyama B, J. Bacteriol. 96(2):567.
112. International Union Against Tuberculosis and Lung Disease. Public Health Service National Tuberculosis Reference Laboratory and the National Laboratory Network, Minimum requirements, Role and Operation in a Low-Income Country. Paris 1998.
113. Iqbal Ahmad, Arina Z. Beg,(2001)Antimicrobial and phytochemical studies on 45 Indian medicinal plants against multi-drug resistant human pathogens, Journal of Ethnopharmacology 74 113–123
114. Ishurda O, John FK. 2005: The anti-cancer activity of polysaccharide prepared from Libyan dates (*Phoenix Dactylifera* L.) Carbohydrate Polymers 59: 531–535.
115. Isoniazidehttp://en.wikipedia.org/wiki/Isoniazid[online] accessed on 31-05-2014
116. Ivan A. Ross, 2005 : Medicinal Plants *of the* World Volume 3 *Chemical Constituents, Traditional and Modern Medicinal Uses* Totowa, New Jersey Humana Press 629pp.
117. Jain RC 1993: Antitubercular activity of garlic oil. 13. Indian drugs 30: 73-5.
118. Jasmer, R.M. Nahid, P. And Hopewell, P.C. 2002: Latent tuberculosis infection.*N.Engl.J.Med.* 347,1860-1866.

119. Javanmardi J, Stushno C, Locke E, Vivanco JM. 2003: Antioxidant activity and total phenolic content of Iranian Ocimumaccessions. Food Chemistry. 83: 547–550.

120. Jensen K. A. 1955: Towards a standardisation of laboratory methods. Second report of the Sub-Committee of Laboratory Methods of the IUAT. Bull Int Union Tuberc 25 (1-2): 89-104.

121. Jensen K. A. Towards a standardisation of laboratory methods. Second report of the Sub-Committee of Laboratory Methods of the IUAT. Bull Int Union Tuberc 1955; 25 (1-2): 89-104.

122. Jigna P., Sumitra V. Chanda 2007: In vitro Antimicrobial Activity and Phytochemical Analysis of Some Indian Medicinal Plants. Turk J Biol, 31, 53-58

123. Jigna Parekh, Darshana Jadeja, Sumitra Chanda 2005: Efficacy of Aqueous and Methanol Extracts of Some Medicinal Plants for Potential Antibacterial Activity Turk J Biol 29 , 203-210

124. Joe M , Bai Y , Nacario RC, Lowary TL. Synthesis of the docosanasaccharide arbinan domain of *Mycobaterial* arabinogalactan and a proposed Otadecasaccharide biosyn-thetic precusrsor. J Am Chem Soc 2007; 129(32) : 9885-9901.

125. Jones, David 2002: "The Health Care Experiments at Many Farms: The Navajo, Tuberculosis, and the Limits of Modern Medicine, 1952-1962". *Bulletin of the History of Medicine* 76 (4): 749–790.

126. Jorge A. Pilheu, Jose A. Iannello, Roberto Bonacossa Torrent and Juan A.Willson 1962: Serum Proteins in Pulmonary Tuberculosis,chest 173-179

127. Joshi S.G 2000: Medicinal Plants pg.11,pg.31.,pg.58.,pg.216,251.

128. Karyadi, E., C.E. West, W. Schultink, *et al.* 2000: A double-blind placebo-controlled study ofvitamin A and zinc supplementation in personswith tuberculosis in Indonesia: effects on clinicalresponse and nutritional status. Am. J. Clin. Nutr.,75: 720-727.

129. Karyadi,E., Schultink, W., Nelwan,R.H.H, et.al. 2000: Poor micro-nutrition status of effective pulmonary tuberculosis patients in Indonesia. *J.Nutr.,130,* 2953-2958.

130. Kaufmann, S.H. 2002: Is the development of new tuberculosis vaccine possible? *Nature Med.* 955-960.

131. Kenneth 2005: Todar University of Wisconsin-Madison Department of Bacteriology)

132. Kenneth G. Zysk, Medicine in Veda, Publisher Motilal Banarsidas, 1998, ISBN 8120814010,pg 12

133. Kent TK, Kubica GP. 1985: Public health mycobacteriology A guide for the level III laboratory. Atlanta, *Center for Disease Control.*

134. Khandelwal K.R. 2000: Khandelwal K.R, Practical Pharmacognosy, 2 nd Edition, 2000; 149 - 56

135. Khare C.P. 2004: Indian Herbal Remedies Rational Western Therapy, Ayurvedic and other Traditional Usage, Botany Springer-Verlag Berlin pg. 5

136. Khare CP 2004: Encyclopedia of Indian Medicinal Plants, Springer-Verlag Berlin, Heidelberg, New York, pp 4

137. Khare CP 2007; Indian medicinal plants, An Illustrated Dictionary. Springer-Verlag Heidelberg, New York, 3-4.

138. King, E.J. and Woott on, I.D.P. 1964: Micro- analysis in Medical Biochemistry. 4th Edition, J&A Churchill, London.

139. Kirtikar KR, Basu BD 1991: Indian Medicinal Plants, Vol 1, New Delhi, India, pp 314.

140. Kochi A 1996: WHO Global Tuberculosis Programme TB : Groups at Risk. WHO report on the tuberculosis epidemic. *Geneva : World Health Organization.*

141. Kothare, S.N. 1959: ABO blood groups in relation to pulmonary tuberculosis. A preliminary report. J. Postgrad. Med., 5: 94-98.

142. Krisanapun C, Peungvicha P, Temsiririrkkul R, Wongkrajang Y. 2009: Aqueous extract of *Abutilon indicum* Sweet inhibits glucose absorption and stimulates insulin secretion in rodents. Nutr Res. Aug;29 (8) :579-87

143. Kurashima K, Mukaida N, Fujimura M, Yasui M, Nakazumi Y, Matsuda T, et al . 1997: Elevated chemokine levels in bronchoalveolar lavage fluid of tuberculosis patients. Am J Respir Crit Care Med 155: 1474-7

144. Laha, P.N. and Dutta, M. 1963: Association between blood groups and pulmonary tuberculosis. J. Ass. Phys. India, 11: 287.

145. Lebrun L, Gönüllü N, Boutros N, *et al.* 2003: Use of INNO-LIPA assay for rapid identification of *mycobacteria. Diagn Microbiol Infect Dis* 46:151–153

146. Lee RB, Li W , Chatterjee D, Lee RE. Rapid structural characterization of the erabino- galactan and lipoerabinomannan in live mycobacterial cells using 2D and 3D HR-MAS NMR; structural changes in the arabinan due to ethambutol treatment and gene mutation are observed. Glycobiology. 2005;15(2) : 139-151.
147. Lehmann, *J. 1946:* Para-aminosalicylic acid in the treatment of tuberculosis. *Lancet 247:15*-16
148. Leonard MK, Osterholt D, Kourbatova EV: how many sputum specimens are necessary to diagnose pulmonary tuberculosis? Am J infect control. 2005; 33(1) :58-61.
149. Letvin, N. L. Bloom, B.R and Hofman, S.L. 2001: Prospects for vaccines to protect against AIDS, tuberculosis and malaria, *JAMA,* 606-611
150. Lim, J. C, Chan, T. K, Ng, D. S, Sagineedu, S. R, Stanslas, J, & Wong, W. S. 2012: Andrographolide and its analogues: versatile bioactive molecules for combating inflammation and cancer. Clin Exp Pharmacol Physiol. 39(3), 300-10.
151. Liu, J, Wang, Z. T, & Ji, L. L. 2007: In vivo and in vitro anti-inflammatory activities of neoandrographolide. Am J Chin Med. 35(2), 317-28.
152. Llesuy S.F and Tomaro M.L. 1994: Heme oxygenase and oxidative stress: Evidence of involvement of bilirubin as physiological protector against oxidative damage.*Biochem. Biophys. Acta,* 12. 239-244.
153. Long, James W. 1991 *Essential Guide to Prescription Drugs 1992.* New York: HarperCollins Publishers. pp. 925–929. ISBN 0-06-273090-8
154. Luisa Jordao and Otilia V. Vieira, 2011: Review Article:Tuberculosis: New Aspects of an Old Disease, Hindawi Publishing Corporation, International Journal of Cell Biology, Article ID 403623, 13 pages
155. M. Muthuswamy, Prabuseenivasan And Vanaja Kumar 2013 Screening Of Antitubercular Activity Of Some Medicinal Plants From Western Ghats, India,International Journal of Pharma and Bio Sciences ISSN 0975-6299 Int J Pharm Bio Sci; 4(4): (B) 328 - 334
156. M.Muthuraj, S. Kamatchiyammal,B. Usharani, S. Manupriya, A.R.Niranjana Ayyappan and K. 2010: Divyalakshm,Serum Zinc, Calcium and Albumin Levels in Pulmonary Tuberculosis Patients Co-Infected with HIV,Global Journal of Biotechnology & Biochemistry 5 (1): 27-35, ISSN 2078-466X
157. Mansouri, A.; Embarek, G.; Kokkalou, E. and Kefalas, P. 2005: Phenolic profile and antioxidant activity of the Algerian ripe date palm fruit (Phoenix dactylifera). Food Chem. 89: 411-420
158. Manu Pant *et.al.* 2010: De novo Shoot Organogenesis from Cultured Root Explants of Swertia chirata Nature and Science 8(9)
159. María A, Hidalgo, Juan L. Hancke, Juan C. Bertoglio and Rafael A. Burgos, 2013: Andrographolide a New Potential Drug for the Long Term Treatment of Rheumatoid Arthritis Disease, chapter 11,Innovative rheumatology,http://dx.doi.org/10.5772/55642,published by INTECH.
160. Maria Teresa Timbal (1925 - 1969) http://archiviostorico.corriere.it /2013/agosto/10/chimico_che_salvo_molte_vite_co_0_20130810_63918b4e-017d-11e3-ae0c-005a4b618eb7.shtml
161. Mathew S, Paramasivan CN, Rehman F, Bolambal R, Rajaram K, Prabhakar R. 1995: A direct rifampicin sensitivity test for tubercle bacilli. *Indian J Med Res* : 99-103.
162. Mathur, J.N. 2002: ICMR Bulletin, August, 32, No.8, ISSN 0377-4910, Indian Council of Medical Research Offset Press, New Delhi-110 029
163. Mc Kinney, J.D. 2002: In vivo veritas; the search for TB drug targets goes live. Nature Med 12,1330-1333
164. McNeill L, Allen M, Estrada C, Cook P. Pyrazinamide and rifampin vs isoniazid for the treatment of latent tuberculosis: improved completion rates but more hepatotoxicity. *Chest* 2003;123:102–106
165. Meyer H, Mally J 1912: "On hydrazine derivatives of pyridine carbonic acids". *Monatshefte Chemie verwandte Teile anderer Wissenschaften* (in German) 33 (4): 393–414
166. Mitra, P.N. 1933: Ind. J. Med. Res., 20 : 995 (1959) J. Ind. Med. Assoc., 33:210
167. Mohamed DA. Al-Okbi SY 2004: In vivo evaluation of antioxidant and anti-inflammatory activity of different extracts of date fruits in adjuvant arthritis. Polish journal of food and nutrition sciences 13; 397-402.
168. Nadkarni K.M, 1976 Dr.K.M.Nadkarni's Indian Materia Medica: Volume 1 Popular Prakashan Pvt. Ltd. Mumbai 1976 pg. 9
169. National TB Institute http://ntiindia.kar.nic.in/aboutus.htm[online] accessed on 31-05-2014

170. New Smear Positive Case Detection Rate, India-2007

171. Nitin S. Bhajipale 2012: Anti-Stress Effect of *Abutilon muticum* in Albino Rats by Swim Endurance Test International Journal of Pharmaceutical & Biological Archives 3(2):368-371

172. Ogunlade, B. L.C. Saalu, O.S. Ogunmodede *et al* 2012: The salutary role of *Allium cepa* extract on the liver histology, liver oxidative status and liver marker enzymes of rabbits submitted to alcohol-induced toxicity Amer. J Biochem. Mol. Biol., 2, pp. 67–81

173. Onyebujoh P, Rodriguez W, Mwaba P. Priorities in tuberculosis research. Lancet 2006; 367: 940-942

174. Palombo,E.A and Samples, SJ. 2007: Antibacterial acitivity of traditional Australian Medicinal Plants, J. of Ethnopharmacology, 77,151-157.

175. Palomino JC, Martin A, Camacho M, Guerra H, Swings J, Portaels F. 2002: Resazurin microtiter plate: simple and inexpensive method for detection of drug resistance in Mycobacterium tuberculosis. *Antimicrob Agents Chemotherap* 46:2720–2722

176. p-aminosalicylic acid (1949), Can Med Assoc J. Mar 1950; 62(3): 231–235. PMCID: PMC1591772

177. Paramasivan C.N. & P. Venkataraman, 2004: Drug resistance in tuberculosis in India Tuberculosis Research Centre (ICMR),Chennai, India, Indian J Med Res 120, October pp 377-386

178. Paramasivan CN 1998: An overview of drug resistant tuberculosis in India. Indian J Tuberc 45 : 73-81.

179. Parichatikanond, W, Suthisisang, C, Dhepakson, P, & Herunsalee, A. 2010: Study of anti-inflammatory activities of the pure compounds from *Andrographis paniculata (burm.f.) Nees* and their effects on gene expression. Int Immunopharmacol. 10(11), 1361-73.

180. Parmar Namita and Rawat Mukesh 2012: Medicinal plants used as antimicrobial agents: A Review, International Research Journal of Pharmacy 3(1) pg 31-40

181. Perkins MD, Roscigno G, Zumla A. 2006: Progress towards improved tuberculosis diagnostics for developing countries. Lancet 367: 942-943.

182. Perry S,Catanzaro. A, Lyashchenko K. P., LoBue P. A., Rendon.A, and Gennaro M. L., 2000: Tuberculosis: Past, Present and Future, p. 44.

183. Pfisterer, P. H, Rollinger, J. M, Schyschka, L, Rudy, A, Vollmar, A. M, & Stuppner, H. 2010: Neoandrographolide from *Andrographis paniculata* as a potential natural chemosensitizer. Planta Med. , 76(15), 1698-700.

184. Porchezhian E, Ansari SH. 2005: Hepatoprotective activity of *Abutilon indicum* on experimental liver damage in rats. Phytomedicine. 12(1-2):62-4.

185. Porth CM. Alteration in respiratory function : respiratory track infections, neoplasm, and childhood disorder. In : Porth CM Kunertmp. Pathophysiology: concept of alter health states. Philadelphia, PA: Lippincott Williams & Wilkins; 2002:615-619.

186. Preparation_of_isoniazid http://commons.wikimedia.org/wiki/File:Preparation_of_isoniazid.png[online] accessed on 19-05-2014

187. Rajalakshmi Padma Vairavasundaram,.and Kalaiselvi Senthil Antimycotic activity of the componenets of *Abutilon indicum* (Malvaceae) Drug Invention Today 2009, 1(2):137 – 139

188. Rajesh F. Udgirkar, Parvin Kadam, Nikhil Kale, Antibacterial Activity Of Some Indian Medicinal Plant: A Review, International Journal Of Universal Pharmacy And Bio Sciences 1(1), Sept-Oct. 2012

189. Rajkumar JS, Sekar MG, Mitra SK. 2007: Safety and efficacy of oral HD-03/ES given for six months in patients with chronic hepatitis B virus infection. *World Journal of Gastroenterology*. 13(30):4103–4107

190. Rakshamani Tripathi, H. Mohan, J.P. Kamat 2005: Rich Radioprotective Profile of Two Indigenous Medicinal Plant *Andrographis paniculata* and *Swertia chirata* Indian Journal of Radiation Research. 10/2005; 2:43-53.

191. Ram VJ, 2001 Herbal preparations as a source of hepatoprotective agents.

192. Ramesa Shafi Bhat and Sooad Al-Daihan 2012, Antibacterial properties of different cultivars of *Phoenix Dactylifera* Land their corresponding protein content Annals of Biological Research, 2012, 3 (10):4751-47-57

193. Rao B.N., Reddy V.D., Sahu P.S., Veerendra Kumar A., David M.A., Yugandhar P., Muralishwar Rao J.2012 ABO Blood Group Distribution and Pulmonary Tuberculosis Journal of Clinical and Diagnostic Research pg1-4

194. Ratnakar P, Murthy PS. 1996: Preliminary studies in the anti-tubercular activity and the mechanism of action of water extract of garlic and its two partially purified proteins. (garlic defensins?). Indian J Clin Biochem 11 : 37-41
195. Ravi Rajurkar et. al. 2009: Anti-inflammatory Action of *Abutilon indicum* (L.) Sweet Leaves by HRBC Membrane Stabilization Research J. Pharmand Tech.2 (2): April.-June.2009
196. Raviglione MC,2006 XDR-TB : entering the post antibiotic era ? Int J Tuberc Lung 2006 : 10; 1185-1187.
197. Renu Gupta *et. al.* 2010: Anti-tuberculosis activity of selected medicinal plants against multi-drug resistant *Mycobacterium tuberculosis* isolates. Source: Indian Journal of Medical Research . Jun, Vol. 131 Issue 6, p809-813. 5p.
198. Reshod A, 1998: Al-Shagrawi. Enzyme activities, lipid fractions, and fatty acid Composition in male rats fed palm pollen grains (*Phoenix dactylifera*). Res. Bult. 79; 5-18.
199. Retimans and Frankel method 1957: This Week's Citation Classic A colorimetric method for the determination of serum glutamic oxalacetic and glutamic pyruvic transaminases. Amer. J. Clin. Pathol. 28: 56-63
200. Revansiddaya P. Biradar Kalyani .Veerangouda.H. Shivkumar., Payghan Santosh 2011: Hepatoprotective and Antioxidant Role of lower Extract of *Abutilon indicum* International Journal of Pharmaceutical & Biological Archives 2(1):541-545www.ijpba.info.
201. Rifampicinehttp://archiviostorico.corriere.it/2013/agosto/10/chimico_che_salvo_molte_vite_co_0_20130810_63918b4e-017d-11e3-ae0c-005a4b618eb7.shtml[online]accessed on 31-05-2014
202. Riska PF, Su Y, Bardarov S, 1999: Rapid film-based determination of antibiotic susceptibility of *Mycobacterium tuberculosis* strains by using a luciferase reporter phage and the Bronx box. *J Clin Mirobiol* 37:1144–1149
203. Riyaz Shaikh, R.L. Manisha, S. Suresh Babu *et al.* 2012: Hepatoprotective activity of alcoholic and aqueous extracts of *Allium cepa* linn. (*liliaceae*) in rats Int. J. Pharm. Sci. Res., 3, pp. 3189–3195
204. RNTCP History http://www.tbcindia.nic.in/history.html[online]accessed on 31-05-2014
205. S.F. Ige, R.E. Akhigbe, O. Edeogho *et al.* 2011 Hepatoprotective activities of *Allium cepa* in cadmium-treated rats Int. J. Pharm. Pharm. Sci., 3, pp. 60–63
206. S.K. Mitra et. al. 1998: Protective effect of HD-03, a herbal formulation, against various hepatotoxic agents in rats Journal of Ethnopharmacology 63 181–186
207. S.K. Mitra, M.V. Venkataranganna, R. Sundaram, S. Gopumadhavan Sharma SK, Mohan A 2004: Extrapulmonary tuberculosis. Indian J Med Res. Oct;120 (4) :316-53
208. Saha R, Ahmed A. 2011: Phytochemical constituents and pharmacological activities of *Acalypha indica*. Int J Pharm Sci & Res 2(8): 1900-04.
209. Saha, N. and Banerjee, B. 1968: Incidence of ABO and Rh blood groups in pulmonary tuberculosis in different ethnic groups. J. Med. Genet., 5: 306-307
210. Saleh FA and Otaibi MM, 2013: Food Processing & Technologyv Antibacterial Activity of Date Palm (*Phoenix Dectylefera L.*) Fruit at Different Ripening Stages J Food Process Technol, 4:12
211. Sampath Kumar K. P., Debjit Bhowmik,Chiranjib,Biswajit,and Pankaj Tiwari 2010: *Allium cepa*: A traditional medicinal herb and its health benefits, *J. Chem. Pharm.* Res. 2(1): 283-291.
212. Sasaki Y. Yamagishi F. Yasi T. Mizutani F. 1999: A case of pulmonary tuberculosis case with pancytopenia accompanied to bone marrow gelatinous transformation. Kekaku. 74 (4):361-4.
213. Seetharam YN, Chalageri G, Setty SR, Bheemachar 2002: Hypoglycemic activity of *Abutilon indicum* leaf extracts in rats. Fitoterapia. Apr; 73(2):156-9.
214. Sen, N. N., Mukerjee, C.L. and Aikat BK. 1959: J. Ind. Med. Assoc., 33:210
215. Shahid Akbar 2011: http://www.academia.edu/4862755/Andrographis _paniculata
216. Shariati, M.; Sharifi, E. and Kaveh, M. 2008: The Effect of *Phoenix Dactylifera* (Date- palm) Pit Powder on Testosterone Level and Germ Cells in Adult Male Rats. J. Zanjan Unversity of Medical Sciences and Health Services Winter ; 15(61):21-27.
217. Sharma D, Cukras AR, Rogers EJ, Southworth DR, Green R 2007: "Mutational analysis of S12 protein and implications for the accuracy of decoding by the ribosome". Journal of Molecular Biology 374 (4): 1065-76.

218. Sharma SK, Mitra DK, Balamurugan A, Pandey RM, Mehra NK. 2002 Cytokine polarization in miliary and pleural tuberculosis.J Clin Immunol 22: 345-52.
219. Sharma SK, Mohan A 2006: Multidrug-resistant tuberculosis: a menace that threatens to destabilize tuberculosis control. Chest 130: 261-272.
220. Sharma, SK; Sharma, A; Kadhiravan, T; Tharyan, P 2013: "Rifamycins (rifampicin, rifabutin and rifapentine) compared to isoniazid for preventing tuberculosis in HIV-negative people at risk of active TB.". *The Cochrane database of systematic reviews*
221. Shivaprakash G., H.N. Gopalakrishna, Deepti Sandeep Padbidri, Shruthi Sadanand, Sahu Sudhanshu Sekhar, R.Shetty Nivedita 2011: Evaluation of *Andrographis paniculata* leaves extract for analgesic activity *Journal of Pharmacy Research 4(10),3375-3377*
222. Simpson DG, Walker JH. Hypersensitivity to para-aminosalicylic acid. *Am J Med* 1960; 29: 297–306
223. Singha PK, Roy S and Dey S. 2007: Protective activity of andrographolide and arabinogalactan proteins from *Andrographis paniculata Nees* against ethanol-induced toxicity in mice. J Ethnopharmacol. 111:13-21.
224. Siti Fairuz Che Othman, Syed Zahir Idid, Mustapha Suleiman Koya, Aisyah Mohamed Rehan, and Kamarul Rahim Kamarudin 2011: Antioxidant Study of Garlic and Red Onion: A Comparative Study, Pertanika J. Trop. Agric. Sci. 34 (2): 253 – 261.
225. Sivakumar A and Jayaraman G. 2011: Anti-tuberculosis activity of commonly used medicinal plants of south India. J. Med. Plants Res. 5: 6881-6884
226. Sivam, G. P., Lampe, J. W., Ulness, B., Swanzy, S. R., & Potter, J. D. 1997. *Helicobacter pylori*—in vitro susceptibilityto garlic (*Allium sativum*) extract. *Nutrition and Cancerology*, 27, 118–121.
227. Smith I 2003: Clinical Microbiology Reviews. 16, No. 3, p 463-496.
228. Snider DE Jr, Kelley GD, Cauthen GM, Thompson NJ, Kilburn JO 1985: Infection and disease among contacts of tuberculosis cases with drug resistant and drug susceptible bacilli. Am Rev Respir Dis 132 : 125-32.
229. Sodeik B, Griffiths G, Ericsson M, Moss B, Doms RW 1994: "Assembly of vaccinia virus: effects of rifampin on the intracellular distribution of viral protein p65". *J. Virol.* 68 (2): 1103–14.
230. Solis, L. A., Shin, S. S., Han, L. L., Lanos, F., Stowell, M. & Sloutsky, A.2005:Validation of a rapid method for detection of *Mycobacterium tuberculosis* resistance to isoniazid and rifampin in Lima, Peru. *Int J Tuberc Lung Dis 9, 760–764*
231. Soumendra Darbar, Anirbandeep Bose, Uttam Kumar Bhaumik, Bikash Roy, Nilendra Chatterjee and Tapan Kumar Pal, 2009: Antioxidant and hepatoprotetctive effect of *Andrographis paniculata* leaf extrat o diclofenac induced hepatotoxicity in rats Pharmacologyonline 2: 95-108.
232. Soundhari C and Rajarajan S. 2013: In vitro Screening of lyophilized extract of alpinia antimycobactrial activity. International Journal of Biological & Pharmaceutical Research. 4(6): 427-432
233. Srinivasan, D. Sangeetha Nathan, Suresh. T, and Lakshmana Perumalasamy, P. 2001: Antimicrobial activity of certain Indian Medicines, J. of Ethnopharmacology, 74,217-220.
234. Stockley, Ivan H. "Anticoagulant Drug Interactions." Drug Interactions. 3rd ed. Boston: Blackwell Scientific Publications, 1994. pp. 274-275
235. Streng and Ryti 1927) string, C. and Ryti, E, 1927: (Spelling) Quoted by Allen, T.M. Brit.Med. Journal ; 2 : 1206
236. Sumathi Muralidhar & Lakshmi Srivastava, 2004: New Delhi, Evaluation of three methods to determine the antimicrobial susceptibility of *Mycobacterium tuberculosis.* Indian J Med Res 120, November, pp 463-467.
237. Surveillance reports : reported tuberculosis in the United State. Centers for disease a. control and prevention 2005
238. T Bando; M Fujimura; Y Noda; J Hirose; G Ohta; T Matsuda *Chest.* 1994; Pulmonary plasma cell granuloma improves with corticosteroid therapy. 105 (5):1574-1575. doi:10.1378/chest.105.5.1574
239. Talwar C.L. and Sawney, C.P.1958: *Ind.J. Med . Science.* 12:942
240. Tandon V. *et al.*, 2005 educational fouram Pleiotropic effects of statins3,72: 77-85
241. Taneja, D.P 1990: Observation on serum zinc in patient of pulmonary tuberculosis.J.Indian Med. Associaltion, 88,280-281.

242. TB elimination: the difference between latent Tb infection and active TB disease. Center for disease control and preventions. Website: **Error! Hyperlink reference not valid.**. Updated October 7, 2008 accessed January 28,2009.
243. tb India 2007/RNTCP Status Report/www.tbcindia.org[online]accessed on 10-05-2014
244. Thamaria J.P.,Mathur K.C And Husain S.A., 1972: Frequency Distribution of ABO Blood Groups among General Population of Northern Rajasthan And among Sputum Positive Pulmonary Tuberculosis cases with particular reference to rate of in-activation of Isoniazid, Ind. J. Tub., Vol. XIX, No. 1,30-33.
245. The Wealth of India, Vol 1, CSIR Publication, New Delhi, India, 2005, pp 21
246. Thomas RG, Dumler SJ, Carlyon JA 2009: "Current management of human granulocytic anaplasmosis, human monocytic ehrlichiosis and *Ehrlichia ewingii* ehrlichiosis". *Expert Reviews in Anti-Infection Therapies* August 7 (6): 709–722.
247. Trease G, Evans WC 1989. Pharmacognosy. 11th edn. Brailliar Tiridel. Can. Macmillian publishers
248. Trivedi NP, Rawal UM 2001: Hepatoprotective and antioxidant property of *Andrographis paniculata* Nees in BHC induced liver damage in mice. Indian J. Exp. Biol. 39:41-46.
249. Tuberculosis bacilli, 1882 http://www.deltaomega.org/documents /RkochAetiology TB.pdf
250. Tyagi SP,Pradhan S, Agarwal SS 1965: Blood groups in malignant disease. J. Ind. Med. Assoc. 45:645-650.
251. Tyagi, S.P., Hameed, S., Bahadur, P., Prasad, M. and Khare, K.B. 1970: Indian J. Med. Res., 58, 596
252. Tyagi, S.P.,Tiagi, O.K. and Pradhan Sushila: 1967: Indian J, Med Sci., 21, 6
253. Tyagi. S.P., Hameed, S. and Jain, K.C 1966: Indian Med. Gaz., 6. 4.
254. Van Der Zanden AG, Te Koppele-Vize EM, Vijaya Bhanu N, Van Soolingen D, Schouls LM. 2003: Use of DNA extracts from Ziehl-Neelsen-stained slides from molecular detection of rifampin resistance and spoligotyping of *Mycobacterium tuberculosis*. *J Clin Microbiol* 41:1101–1108.
255. Vikrant Arya 2011: A Review on Anti-Tubercular Plants.International Journal of PharmTech Research CODEN (USA): April-June Vol. 3, No.2, pp 872-880,
256. Voet, Donald & Voet, Judith G. 2004: Biochemistry (3rd ed.). John Wiley & Sons. p. 1341. ISBN 0-471-19350-X.
257. Walter, U., Luthe, H., Berhart, R. & Soling, H. D. 1975: Eur. J. Biochem. 59, 395-403
258. Weiming C, Xiaotian L. 1982: Deoxyandrographolide-19beta-D-glucoside from the leaves of *Andrographis paniculata* .Planta Med 45 :245-246.
259. White, A. *et al.* 2013 "Evaluation of the Safety and Immunogenicity of a Candidate Tuberculosis Vaccine, MVA85A, Delivered by Aerosol to the Lungs of Macaques." Clinical and Vaccine Immunology 20 : 663-672.
260. Whitemore, B. B., & Naidu, A. S. 2000. Thiosulfinates. In A. S. Naidu (Ed.), Natural food antimicrobial systems *Boca Raton, FL: CRC Press.* pp. 265–380.
261. World health organization World Health Organization.2004 The World health report 2003: changing history. Geneva, Switzerland: 2004.
262. World Health Organization, 2002 Global Tuberculosis Control, WHO Report, Geneva,2002.
263. World Health Organization. 1997 Anti-tuberculosis drug resistance in the world. The WHO/IUATLD Global Project on Anti-Tuberculosis Drug Resistance Surveillance (WHO/TB/97.229). Geneva, World Health Organization Document, 1997.
264. World Health Organization. Global tuberculosis control: a short update to the 2009 report 2009.Doi: WHO/HTM/TB/2009.426.
265. World Health Organization.2004 Anti-tuberculosis drug resistance in the world. Third global report. The WHO/IUATLD Global Project on Anti-Tuberculosis Drug Resistance Surveillance (WHO/CDC/TB/2004). Geneva, World Health Organization document, 2004
266. Wormser, Gary P.; Dattwyler, Raymond J.; Shapiro, Eugene D.; Halperin, John J.; Steere, Allen C.; Klempner, Mark S.; Krause, Peter J.; Bakken, Johan S.; Strle, Franc; Stanek, Gerold; Bockenstedt, Linda; Fish, Durland; Stephen Dumler, J.; Nadelman, Robert B. 2006: "The Clinical Assessment, Treatment, and Prevention of Lyme Disease, Human Granulocytic Anaplasmosis, and Babesiosis: Clinical Practice Guidelines by the Infectious Diseases Society of America". *Clinical Infectious Diseases* November, 43 (9): 1089–1134.

267. Xing, Z., J. Gauldie, G. Cox, *et al.* 1998. IL-6 Is an anti-inflammatory cytokine required for controlling local or systemic acute inflammatory responses. J. Clin.Invest., 101: 311-320.

268. Yamanaka K, Sakai S, Nomura F, Akashi T, Usui T. 2001: A nutritional investigation of homeless patients with tuberculosis. Kekkaku. 76 (4): 363-370.

269. Yasmin S, Kashmiri MA, Asghar MN, Ahmad M, Mohy-Ud-Din A. 2010: Antioxidant potential and radical scavenging effects of various extracts from *Abutilon indicum* and *Abutilon muticum*. Pharm Biol. Mar;48 (3):282-9.

270. Yee D, Valiquette C, Pelletier M, Parisien I, Rocher I, Menzies. Epub 2003 Incidence of serious side effects from first-line antituberculosis drugs among patients treated for active tuberculosis. D.Am J Respir Crit Care Med. 2003 Jun 1;167(11):1472-7

271. Yousif, A. K., N. D. Benjamin, A. Kado, S. M. Alddin and S. M. Ali. 1982 Chemical composition of four Iraqi date cultivars. Date Palm J. 1:285-294.

272. Zaidan MR, Noor Rain A and Badrul AR. 2005: In vitro screening of five local medicinal plants for antibacterial activity using disc diffusion method. Trop Biomed. : 22:165-170.

273. Zia H. Khan1,Shankar S. Warke,, Effect of Antituberculosis Drugs on Levels of Serum Proteins in Pulmonary Tuberculosis Patients, International Journal of Pharmaceutical Research & Allied Sciences, Volume 1, issue 3 (2012), 94-100.

End Of Book

Tuberculosis is a pandemic disease that spreads worldwide. The Revised National Tuberculosis Program-RNTCP is operational in many countries by the World Health Organization-WHO. Tuberculosis has many sad effects both on patients and on the contractual employees working in it. There are employment posts in the project of RNTCP by the local government like Nagpur Municipal Corporation-NMC. These posts included District Programme Coordinator, District PPM (public-private mix) Coordinator, Senior Treatment Supervisor (STS), Senior Tuberculosis laboratory supervisor (STLS), RNTCP Lab Technician/ Sputum Microscopist, Tuberculosis Health Visitor(TBHV), Data Entry Operator. I got an opportunity in 2002 to work in RNTCP as RNTCP Lab Technician. The experiences are inspiring and have many lessons to be learned. The ground situation in the urban area of Nagpur was pathetic during 2002. After joining my duties, I first underwent a short term training program for learning about RNTCP. I learned the program execution of what my role as Laboratory Technician was. I was getting a salary of Rs.5000/- per month. Finally, after training, I reported to the head office at Sadar, Nagpur. Dr Bhawna was my City Tb Officer and my employer. She has a smiling face and in round aspects her eyes are always smiling. I was given the duty to look after two laboratories. One is at the Binaki Mangalwari area, and another is at Budhwari Area. The laboratory had only a platform of stone and a chair. I issued microscope slides, sputum collection vials, Acid Fast Bacillus-AFB staining materials and other related items. I installed everything and started working at the two places - 8 AM to 11 AM in Binaki and 11.30 AM to 2 PM in Budhwari. My job is only to collect samples, process them, examine them and deliver the report as negative-positive with grades like +,++,++ if I saw a bacillus in the slides of samples. In Binaki, the situation was worse as the sweeper used to deliver medicines to patients because the Medical Officer never came on time and if came then only for 1-2 hours. The Nurse, too had the same problem. The charge they collect to see the patient is quite low: Rs. 2 only. Now the Tb patients also started getting suffered due to such an attitude of the Public Health workers ex. Sweeper, Doctor, Nurse. Now I started helping my patients with Tuberculosis as I learned how to give injections with less pain, how to deliver drugs from the box allocated for a specific patient, and, if needed, also render the work of health visitors. The patients were happy with me as I solved their problems instead of avoiding them. There were three categories of patients, i.e. Category I having New Sputum Positive Cases, category II Relapsed/ failure cases, Category III Extra Pulmonary Tuberculosis. Cat I and III have a regimen for six months. Out of that, two months are under observation, and the rest four months is the continuous phase. The treatment is named Directly Observed Therapy (DOT). Category II has an eight-month regimen, out of which three months are under observation and the rest five months are the continuous phase. After every two months for categories I and II, I had to examine the sputum slides of patients for the occurrences of Mycobacterium tuberculosis. The patients were from slums and were too poor to arrange their bread and butter. But still, they feel happy as I used to give injections and if needed the drugs, in addition to my original testing work. After Binaki, I had to go to Budhwari District Tuberculosis Centre-DTC, another laboratory for work. There was also the same problem with the permanent employees non-working or working in a less efficient mode. The permanent laboratory technician used to collect samples till I arrived and all tests and reporting were on my shoulders. So after reaching the lab, I didn't even have time to drink water. But one thing was good that I met Sharma sister there, and she was quite honest in her duties. So I didnot have to administer injections to patients. She was a widow, and she had two small girl kids too. but she was managing the home and lab well. I used to speak with her and bring samosas for her, and we both ate in the afternoon if the patient load was lower. One incident here I am highlighting is a sad event that I will never forget. One night, it rained continuously. The next morning I got ready to go to Binaki. When I reached Binaki lab, I saw that the lab was half-drowned in water. My microscope was also drowned in water. I felt too sad about public health in urban cities like Nagpur and wondered what would be there in villages. Now, as I had to do all the work because nobody was there to help me out, I cleaned the microscope and reinstalled it on the top mount. The sweeper was not doing the job allocated to him, so I had to myself dispose of the used samples to stop Tb spread in society. It was the way I used to work in hardship. Also, there was no salary till grant arrival, so I used to be paid by NMC once in 3 months. Hence I joined a college as a visiting lecturer, and for Rs.100 per day, I managed some extra earnings to fulfil my day to day expenses.

One more story I remember. I am sharing it with you. Initially, when I started my job in Tuberculosis, I used to sometimes be careless while wearing masks and gloves, but one incident opened my eyes and made me frightened too. It was the incident that happened in District Tuberculosis centre in Jagnath Budhwari Nagpur. I reached the lab. The samples were kept on the platform. I started registering them, then made slides, dried and fixed them. Then I applied the Acid Fast Bacilli-AFB staining method in which I covered the smear with a strong carbol fuchsin solution. Then I heated from underneath the slide until steam came from the stain.

After that, I waited for five minutes. Then I rinsed with water. It was then decolourized by 20% Sulphuric acid or 3% acid alcohol until the smear became pale pink. (wait for nearly five minutes). After all these harsh processes, when I put oil on a slide and started watching under the microscope, I saw one bacillus still alive and moving. I saw it for a while for confirmation, and I thought the bacilli, which remain alive after such harsh treatment then, would not be easily able to be killed inside us by medication. That moment I was struck with worry. I remembered a quote of Robert Koch, who first observed Mycobacterium tuberculosis "If the importance of a disease for humanity is measured by the number of fatalities it causes, then Tuberculosis Must be considered much more important than those most feared infectious diseases such as plague, cholera and the like. One in seven of all human beings dies from Tuberculosis. If one only considers the productive middle-age groups, Tuberculosis carries away one-third, and often more." (ref.https://view.officeapps.live.com).

The eradication of Tuberculosis will be possible only when we deliver our duties properly in healthcare; we need to strengthen our Public Health at grassroots levels. Technology needs to be incorporated more in health care.

The research work depicted in the book originally carried out by me but RTM Nagpur University did not awarded me PhD for it after successful pass of Viva Voce. The sad part is that my 15 years wasted in this research now outcome in readers hand will give me some satisfaction.

Printed by Libri Plureos GmbH in Hamburg,
Germany